Eight Powers to Lift You
to Your Full Potential

how
high
can you
soar

JENNIFER ADAMS

BEYOND WORDS
Hillsboro, Oregon

BEYOND WORDS

8427 N.E. Cornell Road, Suite 500
Hillsboro, Oregon 97124-9808
503-531-8700 / 503-531-8773 fax
www.beyondword.com

Managing Editor: Lindsay S. Easterbrooks-Brown
Editor: Emily Han
Copyeditor: Linda M. Meyer
Proofreader: Ashley Van Winkle
Design: Sara E. Blum
Composition: William H. Brunson Typography Services

First Beyond Words hardcover edition March 2019

For information about special discounts for bulk purchases, please contact Beyond Words Special Sales at 503-531-8700 or specialsales@beyondword.com.

Manufactured in the United States of America

10 9 8 7 6 5 4 3 2 1

Library of Congress Control Number: 2018964135

ISBN 978-1-58270-683-2

The corporate mission of Beyond Words Publishing, Inc.: *Inspire to Integrity*

Contents

Introduction: Are You Living a Fulfilled Life?

When you wake up in the morning, what is the first thought that crosses your mind? *Just five more minutes! Why do I have to get out of bed?* Or maybe this sounds more familiar: *I dread going to the office . . . another long day of to-dos. . . . Where is my life going? I feel stuck.*

Whatever your answer, you knew it instantly. We all do, the moment we wake up. We're excited about what's ahead—or we're not. We feel fulfilled, inspired, and ready for the day—or we don't. Maybe, like so many of us, you're stuck somewhere in the middle, powering through your obligations and commitments, going through the motions. But something feels missing. You never seem to experience a genuine sense of purpose and meaning. We all have our off days, but when our off days become what we expect every day, it's time to ask: *Am I living a fulfilled life?*

No matter where you started out in life or where your choices have led you, know that you possess the power to rewrite your story to this point and achieve fulfillment in your next chapter.

No matter where you started out in life or where your choices have led you, know that you possess the power to rewrite your story and achieve fulfillment in your next chapter. You have the ability to transform a life of mediocrity into a life you love—one that suits you to your core. Not anyone else's version of a fulfilling life but *your* unique expression of what most fulfills you.

Why This Book Is for You

Do you know what a fulfilled life looks like for you?

If not, you are not alone; most people don't. For most of my life, I didn't. It wasn't until I paused to ask myself what I truly wanted out of life that I could visualize a dream big enough to encompass my most fulfilling life.

Before you can have a fulfilling life, you have to be clear on what fulfills you. What brings *you* joy? What makes *your* heart happy? Many of us just go through the motions in life: assuming we have no better options, believing our dreams are impossible to achieve, and feeling that we don't deserve success. Every day seems the same as the one before it, and we "relive" each one like in the movie *Groundhog Day*. Some days may be worse, some days a little better, but rarely are there days when we feel inspired, excited, and fulfilled.

So if you don't yet know what you want out of life, or if you do know but feel unworthy of a more fulfilling life than you currently have, then this book is for you.

Do you have a dream?

Perhaps you do. Perhaps you know exactly what your dream is—a dream you can at least visualize, one that *feels* fulfilling. You know what you want to do, where you want to live, or whom you want to be with, but you seem to lose focus, momentum, and motivation before attaining it. Or you put it off for someday. You wait for another New Year's resolution or a day when all the conditions are right. But when you think that perfect moment or that perfect situation has finally arrived and you're ready to tackle the world, something inevitably knocks you off course.

So what do you do? You end up putting your dream on the back burner. And in the back of your mind you feel that your dream was only wishful thinking. You decide it's impossible. It is something you want, but you believe that it's too late for you, or that the timing's not right, or that you don't deserve it. That fulfilling life, dream career, or loving partner is meant for someone else—someone with a (perceived) better background, more money, greater beauty, or better luck—but definitely not you. If you recognize yourself in this scenario, this book is for you.

Does change scare you?

If fear of change is holding you back, together we can fix this! Change of any kind can bring forth self-sabotaging emotions and habits that can stop us in our tracks. We let our fears keep us from accepting personal responsibility and taking action to propel ourselves toward the lives we deserve. A significant portion of this book is dedicated to helping you break free of your holdbacks so you can soar!

The journey you are beginning with this book is about you. It's about the story that got you here, as well as the story you will write for your future.

Do you want to rewrite your story and plan a brighter future?
We all have a story that has gotten us to where we are today. Some stories are inspiring, some are sad, and some are downright transformational. The journey you are beginning with this book is about you. It's about the story that got you here, as well as the story you will write for your future.

To help you better understand the power and transformational nature of the tools I present in this book, it's important that I share some of my own story.

Most people know me today as an entrepreneur and interior designer, a woman with an international home furnishings company and a media presence. However, where I am today is in all respects far from where I started.

I grew up in a small rural town called Gales Creek in a beautiful part of northwestern Oregon, which was considered to be isolated and remote at the time. My dad worked hard, sometimes working two jobs, but still we struggled financially. Raising four children in our modest circumstances meant that my parents had to be resourceful and frugal, to such a degree that our furniture and clothing were either made by my mom or were donated hand-me-downs from members of our church.

Being raised in a very strict religious home environment, I was not allowed to associate with anyone outside of my church community. Therefore, after-school sports activities, dates, dances, and even phone calls from classmates were forbidden.

My mom was incredibly loving and nurturing, but also so fearful that we would be swayed by other influences that she believed outside association with the "world," of any kind, would not be good for us. If someone attempted to call our home, my mom would simply say, "She is not allowed to have phone calls." The next day at school was always so painful, as rumors would fly about what I might have done that was so bad that I wasn't even allowed to talk on the phone. My sister and I were ridiculed frequently. In fact, one of our classmates found me on Facebook a few years ago to apologize for how badly he had treated us all those years ago. Struggling greatly to fit in at school, I always felt like an outcast, an oddball, and I carried this forward with me into my adult years. Having a simple conversation with anyone outside of my family provoked anxiety, so I stayed quiet and small. I was taken along after school and on weekends to go door to door, preaching the faith. I can remember the embarrassment I felt whenever a classmate unexpectedly greeted us at the door to their home, wishing I could disappear. These early experiences would be a deep source of low self-esteem and fear for years to come.

My saving grace was my sister, Erica, who was just seventeen months younger than me. She was my *everything*. The two of us were inseparable, many nights even choosing to sleep in the same bed. She was tall, beautiful, optimistic, lighthearted, and fun. Although I was older, I was four inches shorter, chubbier, less patient, more serious, and the one more inclined to worry.

Among our many childhood adventures, one in particular stands out. I remember that I couldn't wait to turn twelve to be of legal age to pick strawberries in the local fields. To me, earning money represented options and freedom. The day finally came, and berry-picking season was right around the corner. I was super excited! I even planned my wardrobe, designating a special T-shirt. Much to my dismay, my Mom informed me that she didn't feel it would be safe for me to be in the berry fields alone, and that I would have to wait until my sister also turned twelve. Although I now agree with her logic, I was terribly disappointed. Those seventeen months seemed like forever! But finally Erica was of age and we were on our way, riding the berry bus to the strawberry fields.

What I failed to take into account was that making money by picking berries was my dream, not my sister's. Erica would sit on the buckets, eat the strawberries, wander around and talk to people—anything but pick berries. By the end of the first week, she had had enough. She left the berry fields and started to walk home, which would have been at least a ten-mile walk. When the field supervisor figured out she was missing, he left on a four-wheeler to find her; fortunately, she hadn't gotten far. Our mom was called to pick us up, and we were forever banned from the fields. I was devastated. My only hope of making money that summer was dashed! Or so I thought.

My mom occasionally cleaned houses to make extra money, and it dawned on me that I could do the same thing. I desperately wanted something more, and to be independent, which meant making my own money. Once again I coerced Erica into being my partner. We made flyers that included a sketch of a vacuum and our home phone number, and we posted them in the local grocery store. Every day I would listen to the messages on our answering machine in hopes of getting a call . . . and then it finally happened! Someone was interested! Since I wasn't old enough to drive, my Mom took us to the interview, and we got the job!

The wonderful family we worked for probably had no idea how young we were back then, but they saw how passionate I was, and they didn't seem to notice that Erica was once again being dragged along for the ride. Our mom drove us to and from that job every Sunday for several years until I got my driver's license. We charged fifty dollars to clean their entire house. I thought we were making out like bandits. That was twenty-five dollars each, and for only four hours of work! Jackpot! We kept that job for years, and about a year after I graduated from high school, I gave it away—to my mom.

I was cleaning other people's toilets and making their beds long before I became an interior designer and started my own home furnishings company. Although I had no idea at that young age, learning how a home works (down to the details of organization and cleanliness) complemented the skills and resourcefulness I learned from my parents, all of which would foster my ambition, creativity, and eventual career.

Erica and I also held local jobs after school. When we worked at Fred Meyer, a Northwest regional chain of superstores, I was in the apparel department and Erica was in the grocery section. Every night she would sneak over and hide in the clothing racks so we could be together. Did I mention she was the lighthearted, more carefree one? I was worried that we'd both lose our jobs, but she didn't care about that at all. She just wanted to be together; she did the same at school sometimes, skipping her class during my lunch period so we could eat together. Erica taught me a lot about love, compassion, fun, and taking time to enjoy life.

My precious sister Erica was seventeen when she started having terrible migraines that could last for two weeks straight. They wouldn't let up, so she was taken to the emergency room, where she was diagnosed with a fast-growing, malignant brain tumor. This is something I rarely talk about, and tears are streaming down my face just typing these words. Her brain tumor had appeared suddenly, and three short months later she died. My best friend, frankly my only friend, was gone forever.

Reeling from the grief and pain of losing my sister marked a turning point in my life. I had known to my core as a child that I did not fit in at home, and I had long been counting the days until I could get out—with Erica. After losing her, I felt I had nothing left at home, giving me reason to leave as soon as I could. So at nineteen I moved out of my parents' home and left our religion. Unfortunately, I was both naive and ill-prepared to be on my own. I had no idea what I wanted to do with my life. All I knew then was my desperate need to escape my past, and a deep-seated fear of loneliness—the emptiness I felt from losing Erica. Desperate, confused, and terrified of being alone, I made the rash decision to accept a marriage proposal the very week my sister passed away. The marriage was doomed from the start and eventually failed.

When I look back, I see a frightened, insecure young woman who was learning how to stand on her own feet . . . and making one mistake after another. So many of my decisions then, and for several years to come, were driven by my insecurities and fears. Those missteps would evoke feelings of failure, shame, and guilt, causing me to spiral downward into depression.

During that difficult period, when I thought I had hit bottom, two valuable experiences helped me persevere. One was securing my first big-city job in downtown Portland, Oregon. I landed a position as a receptionist for a busy accounting firm, which opened my eyes to a new set of possibilities. Coming from a sheltered life in a small town, it was as if I had landed on a different planet.

At the front desk I encountered people from all walks of life and varying levels of success. Letting my curiosity overtake my insecurities, I questioned as many people who walked through the door as possible! *Where are you from? What do you do? Are you married? What is your family like? How did you get started? What is next for you?* I received fascinating and diverse answers; it was stimulating and inspiring.

That job exposed me to a variety of people and life paths, which is something I am so grateful to have experienced then; it gave me a new awareness that life had options, that I had choices. Hearing other people's stories planted a seed in me to dream and aspire to something more, as well as the realization of how different my life actually was from theirs at the time. Although I desired more, I still didn't yet know what that more looked like for me.

Four years later, out of the blue, I stumbled upon an interior design trade school. It sparked my curiosity, and I decided to go in and get some information from what turned out to be, at the time, a low-cost option to learn a skill set that greatly piqued my interest. The school was the Heritage School of Interior Design. Having participated in many of my parents' home projects growing up, and having spent years as a housekeeper, the school immediately resonated with me. Meeting founder Jan Springer sealed the deal, and I enrolled. Jan became my first mentor; she took me under her wing and equipped me with the tools and confidence to chart a course as an interior designer.

From this fortuitous encounter, I was on my way to something entirely new. I was heading toward a more prosperous and purposeful life, yet I couldn't shake the loneliness and fear that followed me. Everywhere I went, I never felt I fit in. And it was especially apparent in front of my clients. I observed all the big dreams and aspirations they were living, but I never felt deserving or capable of pulling off a dream life for myself. It would be a few more years before my life truly transformed, years in which I gained experience and routinely practiced the tools I am about to present in this book.

I share my background with you in the hope that it will inspire you to be confident, to understand that your past need not predict your future. You can learn from your past and become resilient and fearless. No matter where you came from or where you are today, if you want more for yourself, you absolutely can have it. My life is proof of that.

Looking back, I can appreciate my past and how my family and my upbringing taught me life lessons that have helped me achieve success today: I learned to work hard; to be creative, resourceful, and persistent; and to take responsibility. I also realize, with compassion, that my decision to break free from my limiting beliefs started me on the path to where I am today. My subsequent mistakes and missteps were the very experiences and relevant lessons I needed to learn from.

Through it all, Erica was and will always be my North Star. I remember the many nights Erica and I spent lying on the grass in our backyard, gazing up at the starry sky and pointing out constellations. I also remember our shared love of butterflies, and how enchanted we were by the fluttering of their exquisite wings. To this day, whenever I look up at the stars or see a butterfly, I feel my sister's presence and know that she continues guiding me with unconditional love, giving me the courage to move forward.

With the loss of my sister, I learned what true love is. Although I wish she could be sitting beside me now, I am grateful to have survived that grief and loneliness. I think of her every day, which has been an incredible source of strength for me. When I have a down day or a setback, I look up at the stars. Sometimes, when I need it most, a butterfly will flutter by and I will feel Erica's presence and know I can move through the challenge, that I will be fine, that change is inevitable.

It is from these early experiences, and many others since then, that I have transitioned to living a fulfilled life, which for me is: my dream career, a loving husband and stepchildren, friendships, and a life of abundance; one that offers me the ability to give back and help others. I now have the happy life I had observed in others but hadn't thought I was deserving of—let alone capable of making my reality. To top it off, I recently graduated from Harvard Business School under their flagship Owner/President Management (OPM) program for entrepreneurs and business owners—something that, as a younger person, I hadn't thought was even possible!

Don't get me wrong; I, too, still have daily challenges, but when anyone asks me if I am fulfilled, I can now respond with an unequivocal yes. When anyone asks if I am happy, content, and surrounded by love and friendship, my answer is a resounding YES!

Once I gave myself permission to dream big, acknowledged that I was as deserving as anyone else, and realized that I could accomplish anything I set out to do, my entire life changed.

How did I transform my life? How did I let go of fear and achieve my dreams? The purpose of this book is to share all of this with you! I hope to empower you by presenting the tools I learned to use, so you too can have the life you dream of. Once I gave myself permission to dream big, acknowledged that I was as deserving as anyone else, and realized that I could accomplish anything I set out to do, my entire life changed. I had the power to rewrite my story and forge a more fulfilling future. You deserve this, too—a life that inspires you to wake up with a smile every day!

What to Expect

To get us started, it is important to share with you a set of transformational tools—what I call the Eight Powers—that have created real magic in my life. I collected them along my journey, and I continue to use them today. For centuries, entrepreneurs, athletes, CEOs, artists, and homemakers—people in all walks of life, from all over the world—have used the following eight powers to see their dreams through to fruition.

The Power of . . .

1. Personal Responsibility

2. Dreaming Big

3. Your Mind

4. Vision Boards

5. Intentions and Stepping-Stones

6. Your Words

7. Being Ready and Fearless

8. Resiliency

As my dear friend and mentor Chuck Martin once reminded me, "There is no straight line to success."

Although I now have a life of joy and abundance, I, like everyone else, still sometimes experience worry, fear, and insecurity. I continue to have setbacks and failures, many of which I will share with you. These are the result of life's natural ups and downs, and they happen to everyone, no matter how successful and fearless we appear to be. As my dear friend and mentor Chuck Martin once reminded me, "There is no straight line to success." These few words have stuck with me for years and have helped me greatly in times of trouble or worry.

The key is having these eight powers readily available, practiced, and mastered so that when the unexpected occurs, you can be resilient, bounce back, and continue to progress toward your dreams—plus be better off for it.

Along with the practical tools I will provide in this book, I will also share inspiring excerpts from interviews with remarkable people I respect and admire; individuals who have done extraordinary things with their lives. In various ways, all of them triumphed over adversity. Glenn Stearns and Dr. Connie Mariano overcame extremely difficult childhoods. Mia Noblet faced paralyzing fear to becoming a world record holder at the age of twenty-three. As you read their personal stories and those of others, you will gain real-life-applicable insights into how they, too, have used these same tools to achieve their dreams.

If there is one message you take away from this book, I hope it is this: *No matter where you are today or where you came from, you possess the power to write the next chapter of your life and achieve fulfillment.*

Together, we will get beyond any limiting beliefs and behaviors that could be holding you back. You'll be armed with proven tools that will help you soar and live your best life. You deserve it!

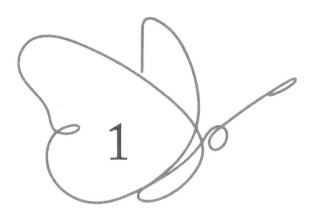

THE POWER
OF PERSONAL
RESPONSIBILITY

If you could kick the person in the
pants responsible for most of your
trouble, you wouldn't sit for a month.
—*Theodore Roosevelt*

During every moment of every day, we are sending and
receiving energy—powerful vibrations we feel within
ourselves and from those around us. You might be exud-
ing joy, fear, love, anger, hope, frustration, or any other emotion.
The energy you give off and take in is a powerful force in your life,

even if you are not conscious of it. You might walk into a packed waiting room and sense the impatience and restlessness of the occupants waiting their turns. Or maybe a colleague walks into your office, takes one look at you, and asks, "What's wrong?" Pets, too, can easily pick up on your mood. My dog will refuse to eat on days when I'm heading out of town. He knows I'm leaving even before I pack my suitcase.

Let's try a quick exercise: Who do you know that exudes joy? Does someone immediately come to mind? Just being around that person is a source of happiness; you sense their positive energy and feel good in their presence. On the flip side, who do you know that exudes tension and anger? I'm sure someone different came to mind. The mere thought of this person is stressful and can bring a reflexive grimace to your face.

The power of attraction is in full force all around you, every second of every day. It is a universal law: you attract more of what you put out into the world.

Taking full ownership of the energy we emit is a critical step in realizing our goals. Owning our energy means taking responsibility for our actions and conduct—how we show up in the world. And that energy is magnetic: like attracts like. The power of attraction is in full force all around you, every second of every day. It is a universal law: you attract more of what you put out into the world.

Your energy originates inside you. It starts with recognizing who you are at your core, your heart center. The person who radiates joy is typically someone who sets their intentions to find joy and gratitude in their life despite the person's past or present circumstances. It's not a gift that someone is necessarily born with; it is probably a conscious, or even subconscious, decision that they made and continues to cultivate in life. We all have that choice, to set an intention of how we want to show up and what we want to attract in our lives.

The law of attraction is beautifully summed up by Lisa Nichols in Rhonda Byrne's *The Secret*:

Everything that you want—all the joy, love, abundance, prosperity, bliss—it's there, ready for you to grab ahold of it. And you've got to get hungry for it. You've got to be intentional. And when you become intentional and on fire for what you want, the Universe will deliver every single thing that you've been wanting. Recognize the beautiful and wonderful things around you, and bless and praise them. And on the other side, the things that aren't currently working the way you want them to work, don't spend your energy faulting or complaining. Embrace everything that you want so you can get more of it.[1]

Your forward movement is fueled by your thoughts and intentions, so the sooner you take ownership of them in every aspect of your life, the closer you will be to achieving fulfillment. We'll continue to explore setting intentions throughout this book, especially in chapter 5, "The Power of Intentions and Stepping-Stones," as I believe they manifest everything we desire.

Taking Ownership of Your Life

Who is responsible for where you are in life right now? Hopefully your answer is, "Me! I am in the driver's seat!"—and you aren't just saying it; you know it to your core. Better yet, you also reflect that sentiment in your actions, as well as the decisions and choices you make on a daily basis.

Taking responsibility for yourself is a critical first step on your journey. It determines how you show up in life and what you attract.

If your answer to the question of who is responsible for where you are in life is anything other than "Me!" or if deep down you feel vulnerable and powerless, know that you are not alone. That is how many of us feel, but we can change it, and doing so is a crucial part of the process of moving toward a fulfilled life. Taking responsibility for yourself is a critical first step on your journey. It ultimately determines how you show up in life and what you attract.

Eckhart Tolle speaks about personal responsibility in his book *The Power of Now*:

If you find your here and now intolerable, and it makes you unhappy, you have three options: remove yourself from the situation, change it, or accept it totally. If you want to take responsibility for your life, you must choose one of those three options, and you must choose now. Then accept the consequences. No excuses. No negativity. No psychic pollution. Keep your inner space clear.[2]

As children we did not have complete control over our decisions, which were often made for us by adults. Usually the only thing you could control was how you reacted to certain situations, although as a kid you probably weren't equipped with the emotional maturity you have subsequently gained through years of life experience in order to react the way you might now.

As an adult, you face choices daily, and you are equipped to make better decisions that can seriously affect your happiness, health, relationships, and career—in short, your future. The sooner you commit to taking charge and being accountable for every aspect of your life, the closer you will be to fulfillment. It is up to you to write your next chapter.

In order to move forward and accept personal responsibility, it is important to shed limiting beliefs you hold about yourself. I know from my upbringing and my past setbacks just how limiting beliefs are planted at a young age and from unhappy, difficult circumstances. We might carry feelings of inadequacy—of not having enough money, not being smart enough, attractive enough, talented enough, or good enough. Held on to as truth, these kinds of thoughts will sabotage our dreams and eventually become our realities.

Conversely, we know there are people who flourish despite an incredibly difficult background or event; they turn adversity into opportunity, and it makes them stronger. As Randy Pausch states in *The Last Lecture*, "We cannot change the cards we are dealt, just how we play the hand."[3] These inspiring people don't let the past stop them from living their best lives. I believe it boils down to the choices they make, and how they continue to take ownership of who they want to be and what they want to achieve. They could have let a negative past experience hold them down, but instead they consciously, or maybe even subconsciously, set their minds and intentions to learn from their adversities and fearlessly move forward.

Glenn Stearns, a friend of mine, endured obstacle after obstacle along his journey to an extraordinarily fulfilled life in love, family, business, and overall prosperity. Had you known only of his past, you probably wouldn't have bet even a dollar on the chances of Glenn's life turning out as well as it has. When I interviewed Glenn for this book, he shared with me that he grew up in a low-income neighborhood in Washington, DC, and faced a series of hardships from an early age. His parents were alcoholics, and school was extremely difficult for him, as he has dyslexia. In fact, school was so tough that he failed fourth grade. And then, at the painfully young age of fourteen, Glenn fathered a child.

With dogged perseverance—and while raising his daughter—he managed to graduate from high school, although in the bottom 10 percent of his class. No one expected much from Glenn's life at that point. Despite these challenges, and seeing many of his friends get mixed up with drugs and be sent to prison, Glenn knew deep down that he was destined for more. He sought guidance from a series of mentors who helped him gain the confidence and motivation to go after a better life for himself and his family.

Glenn went on to graduate from college and then moved to California, where he waited tables until he began working as a loan officer. At the age of twenty-five he created his own mortgage company, Stearns Lending, LLC. Fast-forward a few decades, and Glenn won the prestigious Ernst & Young Entrepreneur of the Year Award and grew his company to nearly $1 billion in funding per month despite the 2007 mortgage crisis, emerging as a top lender in the country.

With all this financial success, Glenn has never lost sight of his journey or the importance of giving back. He and his wife, Mindy, are commendable philanthropists and mentors. They created a mentoring leadership retreat called "Surviving and Thriving," and in 2011 Glenn became the youngest member of the Horatio Alger Association of Distinguished Americans, which provides millions of dollars of needs-based scholarships to thousands of American students. Membership in this association is given in recognition of individuals who have achieved personal and professional success despite challenging starts in life. Among others, Oprah Winfrey, Colin Powell, Maya Angelou, and Hank Aaron have also been honored with this award.

Recently Glenn faced cancer, but in true Glenn form, he is "surviving and thriving" under the loving care of his brilliant wife Mindy (who has her own amazing story!). It's hard to believe someone can possess this level of resiliency and determination to create a beautiful life for himself and his family, but Glenn is living proof.

Like Glenn, you are faced with choices and decisions on a daily basis. Some are minor and may feel routine, but others are more significant and can greatly influence what lies ahead. Release your past and take ownership of your future.

POWER MOVE

Identify and reflect on limiting beliefs and behaviors that could be holding you back from a more fulfilled life right now:

- *List your limiting beliefs and behaviors in your journal.*

- *Can you trace the source of a particular belief or behavior? Write down its story. It may be painful to remember, but by doing so, and especially by writing it down, you take action to release yourself from its hold.*

- *Take time to reflect. Circle back to this Power Move as you continue through this book, adding to your list and your stories as you learn more about yourself and your holdbacks.*

Following are examples of other areas we can own—take personal responsibility for—that support a more satisfying life. I highlight them now with a set of self-reflection questions, and following chapters will discuss each one in greater depth. While reading through this list, you will want to reflect on your own life and determine the areas that apply to you, the areas in which taking more personal responsibility could help propel you closer to the life you want.

Own Your Time

Oftentimes it's easier to put ourselves into harm's way by overcommitting, simply because we don't want to offend someone, when really we should have said no. It can be hard to refuse someone you don't want to spend time with, or to decline an activity that, while you might find a way to cram it onto your already-packed calendar, would wreak havoc on your stress level. These unhealthy habits have a ripple effect on how you interact with your family, your coworkers, and yourself, let alone leaving you less space to focus on your personal growth and dreams. A shift in your behavior—taking control over every commitment you make—is crucial to cultivating a fulfilled life. Remember, "no" is a complete sentence and a perfectly acceptable answer.

> The essence of the best thinking in the area of time management can be captured in a single phrase:
> *Organize and execute around priorities.*
> *Stephen Covey*

Simple shifts in how you use your time can have a big effect in every area of your life but particularly your health, relationships, and success. Practice and master the art of balancing your time and learning to use it wisely. Time is a precious resource that deserves to be cared for. Overcommitting, rushing around, and always being busy does not support a satisfying life.

Since starting to manage my time, I now make a point *not* to use the excuse, "I am too busy." I am present and aware of my obligations, which has enhanced my level of happiness and my life as a whole. I now make time-related choices by asking myself: *Is this something I want to do? Is it aligned with my life intentions?* If the answer is yes, then I will commit to it.

A shift in your behavior—taking control over every commitment you make—is crucial to cultivating a fulfilled life.

We can find time if we sincerely want to. For example, somehow I am blissfully finding time to write this book in the midst of running a demanding business and entering my final month of business school before graduating. Writing this book is something I have dreamt of for years! It's aligned with my personal definition of a fulfilled life, and it brings me immense joy . . . and somehow the time has miraculously opened up for me. All my other commitments and obligations are being addressed too. How is this possible, you ask? I learned the art of saying no. I consciously say no to things that add distraction and don't bring me joy. If someone had asked me a year ago if I had the time to write a book under these circumstances, I would not have believed I could make it happen. Yet here it is.

Now that I intentionally prioritize my time, I have learned to say a simple no, or if the situation warrants, I'll say: "At the moment it won't work for me, but it's something that I'd love to do eventually, and I'll let you know when I can." By taking ownership of my time, I take charge of what's important to me in the present moment, being mindful of my intentions and how I want to show up. "I am just so busy right now" sounded as if I were a victim to a schedule that was out of my control, and being a victim is not who I want to be. We are responsible for our time and our lives in general, and we should let our commitments reflect this.

POWER MOVE

Reflect on how you manage your time. Ask yourself:

- *Will this request, invitation, opportunity, or activity move me closer to my life goals and aspirations, or is it a distraction?*

- *Are my choices and time management aligned with my priorities and intentions?*

It's so easy to fall into the time trap of browsing online or on social media feeds. It is a surprisingly addictive way to subconsciously check out. This can be a major distraction from all that we desire to do with our time. An insightful observation came from author and mom Manoush Zomorodi:

My mind felt tired. Worn-out. Why? Yes, I was juggling motherhood, marriage, and career in one of the most hectic cities in the world. But it was more than that. In order to analyze what was going on with me, I began by observing my own behavior. What I found was, frankly, exhausting. As soon as I took a moment to reflect, I realized there wasn't a single waking moment in my life that I didn't find a way to fill—and my main accomplice was my phone.[4]

It is much easier said than done, but if you set an intention for yourself to limit these distracting activities, even if only temporarily by doing a digital detox while you're charting the next phase of your life, it'll become much easier to catch yourself in the act and course correct before a few minutes turn into wasted hours.

> When it comes to social media—
> there are just times I turn off the
> world, you know. There are just some
> times you have to give yourself space
> to be quiet, which means you've got to
> set those phones down.
>
> *Michelle Obama*

Only you can control what goes on your calendar and how you spend your days. Running around feeling frustrated (*There aren't enough hours in the day!*) does not attract more time to your life. Pausing to reflect on how you use your minutes, hours, and days, and mindfully making choices around that, will bring you more of the time you need. Doing so will also bring you more joy, as you are ultimately taking ownership.

Own Your Part

It's much easier to blame someone else for an outcome that isn't to our liking, as opposed to owning our parts in a given situation. This can be especially challenging when a relationship has gone bad, whether personal or professional.

For example, I recently hired a landscaper to install new plants in my yard. I walked by one section out front and thought, *What was he thinking? Those should have gone in the backyard!* At the outset, I could have taken the time to give him direction, and in fact, he had asked me for it, so there was no one to blame but myself.

When any kind of relationship is a struggle, it's much easier to focus on the other person's flaws and fixate on what they did wrong: how they mistreated you, what a horrible person they are, or how badly they disappointed you, as opposed to looking at the role you played in the demise of the relationship or the situation. Being able to own our parts is the source of real power and real peace.

Instead, we can fall prey to wasting our time and energy by telling that person off inside our heads. We allow negativity and blame to fill our minds and bodies until that energy is all we radiate. Is that negativity what you want to exude to others? Is that the state of mind that will help you live your best life?

I believe we are presented with opportunities that can help us grow and learn, chances to reflect on what we could have done differently in a given situation. If you can shift your mental focus to owning your part in the relationship, it's amazing how much headspace will be freed up to bring forth something positive. You want to shake that negativity as quickly as you can before it takes hold and starts to become what you are.

In my company, every time a relationship with an employee ends, whether it's my choice or the employee's, my board reminds me: *Look first to yourself.* Every single time! *What could you have done differently in this instance, and what will you do differently the next time?* They turn it into a learning opportunity. It's not typically the first thing I want to hear in these situations, but it brings me back to personal growth and the takeaway that I'll be better for it in the next hire.

POWER MOVE

Reflect on the relationships in your life, both personal and professional.

- *Identify where you might be blaming someone else for an outcome.*

- *Where can you take more personal responsibility? What valuable learnings are there to be gleaned from the relationship?*

Relationships are two-way streets. They offer powerful opportunities for learning and personal growth when you practice self-reflection and take responsibility for your role and your actions.

Possibly you have identified a relationship or situation that you're in right now that could be improved simply by taking more personal responsibility. Lucky you! You now have the ability to affect that relationship for the good! On the other hand, if you are in a negative relationship of any kind, and taking more personal responsibility is not going to help the situation, then you must reflect, look at your options, and take healthy action for yourself— even if it means exiting the relationship. That is the one part of any negative relationship that you can control. Get rid of the bad energy to clear space for the good energy and for healthy relationships to flow more freely to you.

Own Your Work

Whatever your work or profession, whether you are a teacher, carpenter, designer, executive, homemaker, or artist, you have the opportunity to do and be your best. It can help if you're doing work you love, but even if you're not at this time, you still have the choice to show up with the right attitude. Or choose to get out of it altogether. Complaining about it does no good; it only spews negative energy at everyone you encounter, which is not fair to anyone. Continually grumbling about your job yet doing nothing to improve it does not allow positive energy to flow freely back to you.

There was a time before I transitioned my design services business model into a product development model when I was *so* burned out. It got so bad that, although I had what most outsiders perceived as a dream job, I couldn't have cared less about picking out another paint color for someone else's home, and when it came time to accessorize with the finishing touches, I was really ready to check out. I'll never forget a dear friend of mine, who was then a client, sensing my burnout and saying, "Remember, your business reputation lies on finishing just as strong as you started." That hit me hard, but a light bulb went off. I was no longer doing work that fueled my passion. I was done before I started! It was time for me, once again, to pause, take a look inside, and evolve into the next phase of my growth. How I did this, I will get into more deeply in the coming chapters.

Own your work and your talents. And if you're not in a type of work that you love, one that showcases your skills, then that's an invitation to take ownership and make your dream job a reality.

Ask yourself: *Do I work from a place of passion, dedication, and initiative?* People present themselves and their skills in different ways and with different attitudes. Own your work and your talents. And if you're not doing work that you love, work that showcases your skills, then that's an invitation to take ownership and make your dream job a reality. This book will help you do that.

Remember, it's up to you to shift your behavior and your patterns of thinking to effect positive change. If, after deep reflection, you've tried everything you can think of and your work situation is still not improving, then it is your responsibility to make a change in your employment or career. And it might just mean making a subtle shift. No one else can do this for you. What you do for work can have an enormous effect on how fulfilled you feel, and on the attitude you project to others. Only you can attract the positive energy that you deserve in your life.

POWER MOVE

Reflect on your current job.

- Are you just showing up? Or are you showing up as your best self?

- Are you blaming someone else because you cannot seem to get ahead in your current role?

- Can you assume greater responsibilities in order to excel and increase your sense of job satisfaction?

Own Your Opportunities

Opportunities come in many guises. Believe it or not, they often arise from what we perceive as loss. We all experience losses and setbacks; it's what we do with them that predicts our ability to build a better future for ourselves. There is much to be learned from a lost opportunity. If you shift blame to the other party and chalk it up as a lost cause, you are missing an invitation to become stronger and more competent at facing life's natural flow of ups and downs. If you listen closely and pay attention to what you could have done better and what you can learn from the situation to be better moving forward, that's when you become wiser, more resourceful, and more deeply committed to achieving a yes on the next try. This applies to anything in life: friendships, love, circumstances, business, and hobbies.

Take personal responsibility and identify the gifts given by every seemingly missed opportunity.

Work hard to identify what went wrong. For example, try to determine what objection the other party had to your proposal, and reflect on what you can do to overcome it the next time you make your pitch. Or reflect on what mishaps you've had while trying to achieve anything in your life, and decide how you will learn from the experiences and be better off as you continue to evolve. In doing so, you can take advantage of losses and setbacks, and use your learnings to drive you forward in your next undertaking. Setbacks are valuable tools for personal growth, fostering courage and resilience.

POWER MOVE

Reflect on a lost opportunity, or possibly multiple lost opportunities.

- *What learnings can be gleaned from the lost opportunity?*

- *Once you have identified your learnings, list the actions you need to take, now or in the future, to propel you toward a better outcome in the next such situation.*

Learnings gained from lost opportunities are special gifts and can offer you an advantage the next time the situation arises. When you pause to identify these gifts, you will be better equipped to create your desired outcome. Don't let these opportunities go to waste. Take personal responsibility and identify the gifts given by every seemingly missed opportunity or circumstance that didn't go your way.

Own Your Intuition

We all have an inner compass, frequently referred to as our gut feeling or intuition. To avoid going wrong, pay attention to your intuition. Watch for warning signs or red flags as they pop up along the way. If your gut tells you something is not right, it most likely is not right. Take personal responsibility for listening to what your intuition is telling you, and don't allow someone else to talk you into believing otherwise. Take the time needed to validate your feeling before proceeding further with the situation or relationship.

In my earlier years, still deeply believing that everyone else I encountered was much smarter than I was, I entered into a real estate transaction that I *knew* to my core was not a good deal, yet I didn't want to disappoint the other person, so I stayed in. There were many times I could have backed out without any harm being done to either of us. Yet I let the fear of disappointing someone else take priority over my gut feelings and, in the end, paid dearly for it. And I only had myself to blame.

Your gut feelings are gifts. It's what we do with them that makes all the difference in our outcomes, and ultimately our reality.

Your gut feeling can also alert you to your deepest, most fulfilled life path. Your intuition is a gift!

Your gut feeling can also alert you to your deepest, most fulfilled life path. Your intuition is a gift! It's a personal power that can guide you to your best choices, your best life, and the fulfillment of your wildest dreams. When you have a deep longing inside, do you sit with that and allow it in? Or do you brush it away, feeling the timing isn't right or that you're not worthy of a life path that is aligned with your deepest yearnings?

If you allow yourself to sit with your gut feeling, even if only for a moment, it will give you the answer you seek and guide you to where you should go. But it takes practice and dedication to trusting your instincts, to truly allowing them in. My gut feeling on what I wanted in my love relationship and in my business scared me at first. It all seemed so lofty! Yet listening to my gut ultimately brought me to my most fulfilled life. I've come to realize that gut feelings are offerings bestowed upon us when we need them most. Cherish them for the gifts that they are.

POWER MOVE

When you get a gut feeling, good or bad, take time to identify it and let it in. Ask yourself:

- *What personal action or course correction is needed to take full advantage of what my intuition is telling me?*

- *When a red flag of intuition arises, do I typically pay attention to it? Or do I brush it off and go with the flow, not wanting to upset anyone?*

- *When a green light shows up, do I allow my intuition to guide me?*

Own Your Well-Being

Your complete well-being, physical and emotional, makes an enormous difference in your ability to be the best version of yourself. Even small shifts in your intentions, followed by personal accountability for your health and fitness, will greatly affect the flow of your life goals coming to fruition, especially your happiness.

Ignoring our well-being means missing an opportunity to experience clarity, joy, and a more pain-free body. Instead of proactively addressing our health concerns, we react to all that life piles on; we tell ourselves we'll start taking better care on any other day than today. We can allow ourselves to go through life feeling tired and sluggish, always in a fog, or we can take personal responsibility and determine why this is happening. Take the time to identify the underlying issue or issues, whether it be lack of sleep, lack of exercise, or poor eating habits. Or possibly you need medical care that you've been putting off for far too long. It's up to you to do the work. Taking healthy action can have an incredible impact on your effectiveness and happiness in all areas of your life.

When you own your well-being, you are acknowledging to yourself and to the world: I am worth it! I deserve to be fit and happy!

When you own your well-being, you are acknowledging to yourself and to the world: *I am worth it! I deserve to be fit and happy!* Remember, your state of mind and body are your own, so who you want to be begins with self-reflection and making choices that will support the life you want.

We all have tired days, and for some of us those days can turn into months, even years! But to be the best version of ourselves, we need to muster up the determination to take complete charge of our wellness, which includes being well rested. Can you change your nighttime patterns in order to get to bed earlier? Or improve your bedroom sleep environment to help you get a better quality of sleep each night? Along with our diet, sleep is a powerful force.

It supports our decision-making abilities, our productivity, the way we feel, our weight, our hormones, and the energy we exude to everyone around us. Sleep can even make a person look more beautiful. The difference between a well-rested person and someone who has not gotten the sleep they need is often readily—and visibly—apparent.

When I was younger, I overheard someone saying they didn't need more than four hours of sleep. So, naively, I used to take pride in trying to see if I could get by on just four to six hours of sleep, as I thought that meant I was strong and efficient with my time. Boy was I wrong! The moment I prioritized sleep in my life, getting the healthy amount of hours I needed, everything else shifted for the good: my relationships, my productivity, my energy, and especially my wellness.

Our food choices matter, too, not only to our physical fitness but also to our brain clarity. A study by Harvard Health states:

> Like an expensive car, your brain functions best when it gets only premium fuel. Eating high-quality foods that contain lots of vitamins, minerals, and antioxidants nourishes the brain and protects it from oxidative stress—the "waste" (free radicals) produced when the body uses oxygen, which can damage cells.
>
> Unfortunately, just like an expensive car, your brain can be damaged if you ingest anything other than premium fuel. If substances from "low-premium" fuel (such as what you get from processed or refined foods) get to the brain, it has little ability to get rid of them. Diets high in refined

sugars, for example, are harmful to the brain. In addition to worsening your body's regulation of insulin, they also promote inflammation and oxidative stress. Multiple studies have found a correlation between a diet high in refined sugars and impaired brain function—and even a worsening of symptoms of mood disorders, such as depression.[5]

Take responsibility for poor food habits, such as overconsumption of fake foods or foods high in sugar or other ingredients that invoke an inflammatory or allergic response. Also, paying attention to the foods that work well for you—in combination with exercise—can be pivotal to clearing brain fog, so you can be better equipped to focus on your important life goals.

Finding a form of physical activity to get daily movement doesn't mean you have to run or do yoga, if neither of those activities is something you enjoy. The key is to identify what types of activities you *do* enjoy . . . and then do them regularly! Even walking around the block a few times during your lunch break every day will change your health for the better.

Quieting your mind can also have a positive effect on your well-being. Meditation is one option for relaxing when your mind is on overload, but find what works for you, and practice it regularly: prayer, quiet walks, or sitting outside in a calming spot and being still for ten minutes, maybe even listening to music that relaxes you. The point is to explore and find what works effectively for *you*, so you can quiet your mind and find peace in times of need. We'll talk more about ways you can quiet your mind in chapter 3, "The Power of Your Mind."

POWER MOVE

Reflect on your overall well-being.

- In what areas of your health are you not yet taking complete personal responsibility?

- What shifts in your behaviors and patterns do you need to make in order to take full responsibility for your health, fitness, and mental well-being?

Own Your Finances

If your current career path is not providing the lifestyle you want and need, you are the only one who can make the choice to identify a different path and work toward a career that will offer the financial stability and freedom you desire. Continually complaining that you are broke and feeling trapped will not fix anything. Allowing yourself to fixate on negative energy when it comes to money definitely won't draw more money to you.

Identifying your path to financial freedom is easy to put off simply for fear of making a change. Catch yourself saying, *I don't know what I want to do*, or *I'm not really good at anything*, or *I'm broke!*—as if this is a permanent situation that you're stuck with and it's out of your control. These are limiting beliefs and patterns that you can control. These might be your current situations or circumstances, but they are not your lifelong disabilities, unless you believe them to be.

When I graduated from high school, my dad had only seventeen dollars in his checking account. Not even enough for us to go out for pizza as a family. However, he then identified a career path that could meet his financial goals, went back to school, and started his own business. He figured out a way to retire comfortably at age sixty-five, pay off his mortgage in full, and even have enough saved to travel and explore the opportunities and experiences that he'd dreamed about. The transformation is remarkable! He always said he would retire at sixty-five, and setting that intention early on definitely paid off for him. We'll talk about how to set goals in all areas of your life, including your finances, in chapter 5, "The Power of Intentions and Stepping-Stones."

POWER MOVE

Reflect and identify where you could take more personal responsibility in the area of your finances.

- Are you putting off a career change out of fear, when ultimately a change is needed in order to position yourself for a life of financial freedom?

- What small shifts can you make to your finances that would help you move closer to a fulfilled life?

Knowing our incomes and expenses and keeping track of our overall financial pictures are generally within our power to control. But as many of us know, setting a budget is not the same as sticking to it; that's where willpower comes in. Are there simple shifts you can make in your spending habits now that you will thank yourself for in the future? Perhaps packing a lunch for work instead of eating out every day? Or using an at-home espresso maker in lieu of daily Starbucks runs? These needn't be permanent sacrifices, as in this book you'll learn how to attain your dream life (which might include daily lattes at Starbucks!). But in the meantime, simple shifts in spending can make a big difference as you take responsibility for choosing a career path that will satisfy your deepest financial desires.

Own Your Choices

The sooner you wrap your head around the fact that your daily choices and intentions do matter, and that the more you take ownership of in your life—relationships, time, wellness, finances, work, and even your speech and your thoughts—the more progress you will make toward your goals. Take ownership of where you are today and where you want to be tomorrow. Let go of the blame, and instead become accountable. This is the way to move forward toward your most fulfilled life.

We often need others to help us along our path to goals, but only you can change your life. No one else can do this for you. You are powerful, and the sooner you release limiting beliefs and behaviors that could be holding you back, the better off you will be.

The personal responsibility part is not always the fun part, but it is a critical first step, and it is well worth the effort it takes to identify some of your holdbacks. We can all identify with something from this chapter, so don't beat yourself up over what you have learned about yourself. The good news is that we have the ability to proactively change, create, and attract our best lives!

POWER MOVE

Reflect and ask yourself these questions:

- Do I give off the type of energy I want to attract?

- Am I solely blaming someone else for something that didn't go my way?

- Has my gut been telling me something, and I've been ignoring it?

- Where can I take more personal accountability to improve a situation or a relationship in my life?

THE POWER OF
DREAMING BIG

What would you attempt to do if you
knew you could not fail?

Robert H. Schuller

For a moment, try to visualize your ideal life situation without any mental restrictions. Remove every "should" or "shouldn't" that you've ever been told, or that you've told yourself. Ignore your current financial situation. Set aside limiting beliefs you have about yourself, where you came from, and where you currently live. Forget about your current job and your current relationships, as well as your hobbies or weekend pastimes.

You might find that practicing this visualization is challenging at first, but hang in there, do your best, and take some calming breaths as you go. Here are some inspiring words to consider from Marianne Williamson:

> Our deepest fear is not that we are inadequate. Our deepest fear is that we are powerful beyond measure. It is our light, not our darkness that most frightens us. We ask ourselves, "Who am I to be brilliant, gorgeous, talented, fabulous?" Actually, who are you *not* to be? . . . Your playing small doesn't serve the world. . . . We are all meant to shine, as children do. . . . It's not just in some of us; it's in everyone.[6]

The pure potential of you. The clean slate to ask yourself, What do I want from my life?

When you feel like you've been able to let go of your limiting beliefs and current life situation, you might find yourself thinking, *What's left?* Well, what's left is pure potential. The pure potential of you. The clean slate to ask yourself, *What do I want from my life?* It wasn't until I asked myself this question that everything in my life dramatically changed.

Permission to Dream Big

Like most of us, I was the queen of putting limiting restrictions on myself. Even when my interior design business started to do well, I looked happy and successful on the outside, yet I didn't feel fulfilled and genuinely happy. Why, you ask? Because I was working and making all my life choices based on the deep-seated fear of going back to a life I knew I didn't want. And subconsciously, I didn't feel worthy of giving myself permission to consider what it was I wanted in the first place!

My holdbacks didn't allow me to believe that I deserved success or that I was worthy of happiness. That fear came from the same belief I had as a kid in school: that everyone else deserved to be happy because they were better than me, and just like back then, even as an adult, I still didn't feel like I fit in. I didn't fit into my old life, or my new life. This belief was paralyzing, and because of it, I was continually (and unknowingly) making compromises and giving up my power. I went along with what others wanted, putting other people's expectations and happiness over my own. This all came to a head when my personal life unraveled with a painful divorce.

If you don't feel fulfilled . . . give yourself permission to expand your vision and dream bigger than your current circumstances.

There's a saying that "when you hit rock bottom, you are open to the greatest change." From the outside, no one would have suspected I had hit bottom, but on the inside I was at a low point in my life. But during that challenging period I made my grandest discovery: the art of dreaming big. I finally woke up to the realization that I had nothing to lose and everything to gain. I had reached my tipping point—it was all or nothing. I was tired and fed up with what was, and I was ready to begin anew with a big change.

As I wrote earlier, it wasn't until I could see myself as pure potential and ask *What do I want from my life?* that I could finally set myself free to concoct my most outlandish dreams of a fulfilling life. And when I did, that's when the doors opened wide for me and miracles happened—opportunities that I would not have thought possible!

If there is one message I hope you take away from this chapter, it is that if you don't feel fulfilled, if you're at a low point like I was, you *do* have options. But only you can give yourself permission to expand your vision and dream bigger than your current circumstances. It's also important that your dream be what you want, not what your family, neighbors, or coworkers want and will validate—nor even what I want. What makes *your* heart soar?

> Your calling isn't something that somebody can tell you about. It's what you feel. It is a part of your life force. It is the thing that gives you juice. The thing that you are supposed to do. And nobody can tell you what that is. You know it inside yourself.
>
> *Oprah Winfrey*

It's time to get real with yourself, even if at first it makes you feel uncomfortable or guilty. You must do it anyway! At this point you don't even have to have a clue as to how you will get there! We'll work on that later.

Dreams can go against the status quo (chart your own course!) or they can be utterly conventional. The key to dreaming big is that the dream is authentically yours, and not to be compared with anyone else's.

What Is a Big Dream?

Dreams and goals mean different things to different people, and there is no right or wrong way to dream big. Dreams take all forms, and they can, and probably will, change and evolve throughout your life. Dreams can go against the status quo (chart your own course!) or they can be utterly conventional. The key to dreaming big is that the dream is authentically *yours*, and not to be compared with anyone else's.

You might dream of traveling to exotic destinations or to a humble cabin in the woods. Perhaps you yearn to spend more of your time helping others. You might have dreams about sharing your life with a romantic love, or perhaps you desire solitude. Maybe you want to have a dream home that's filled with family and friends. Is there a mountain you want to climb? Or a race you'd like to run? A business you want to start? All of these are dreams!

Don't let age, income, or any other current life circumstance get in your way during this process. My mom has shown me the greatest example of this. She is now nearly seventy and lives in a very remote, poverty-stricken area of Africa. She found a way to get beyond her limited resources and follow her heart's desire to dedicate her entire life to giving back to others, doing what brings her great joy: teaching them about the Bible. And I have to say, she is truly the most happy, joyful, and positive person I know. It's really inspiring to me. It's her dream, and although it may be different from mine, that's what makes it so beautiful.

To identify your dreams is to give your life purpose. It's easy to drift from one thing to the next without having a plan for your life. When you hone in on what you really want, you experience your heart's deepest desires, which brings more meaning and direction to your life.

When I first started dreaming big I had to sit by myself and think back on moments when I felt great joy and inspiration. The moments where time just flew by, and everything seemed effortless. Early on in my dreaming-big process I remembered a road trip my family took in my mom's Chevy Nova. Six of us piled into the car for what turned into a twenty-four-hour road trip to visit my aunt. It was our first big road trip out of town from Gales Creek, Oregon, to San Diego, California! It was a huge event for us. And despite the long hours on the road, I was so excited to have this adventure. I will never forget the moment we pulled off the I-5 freeway and onto the Del Mar Heights Road exit. We turned right . . . and there it was . . . the California coastline . . . the sunshine . . . the palm trees . . . everything I had heard about and had seen in magazines but had not experienced in real life.

I can still remember the scent from my aunt's condo the moment we walked in the front door. I can even picture the exact layout of her home. That was a pivotal and memorable journey. As an adult I held that memory close; it was pure joy. It created a lasting impression and a deep desire in me to have a home in San Diego. So once I gave myself permission to dream big, San Diego went on my list. And once I did that, it ended up happening for me much sooner than I ever would have anticipated.

POWER MOVE

Reflect and discover what your big dreams might be. Ask yourself:

- What moments of pure joy resonate with me?

- What were some times in my life when I felt deep purpose? What activities was I engaged in? What kind of place (physical or emotional) was I in?

- Draw upon those moments to look for clues into ways that I can make these happy experiences my daily reality, thus identifying a big dream for myself.

Many times in life, we feel internal conflicts—multiple paths that call to us. This is especially so for women as many feel the pull between a professional life and motherhood. Sometimes the path of the unknown is where our hearts are leading us, but it's scary because we're not in control and that leap makes us vulnerable. One of my dear friends, Cindy Mulflur, had charted a successful career as an investment broker in the stock market. She was in her early thirties and making over six figures with a promising future in the financial industry. Yet she had a different dream—her deepest desire was to have a life at home and be a full-time mom. And she decided to follow her heart.

Now twenty-five years down the road, Cindy recognizes that although she missed the power lunches and many aspects of her career, she experienced not only joy as a full-time mom but also fulfillment. She realizes that regardless of whatever industry boards she might have served on, or whatever income she might have made, she wanted her legacy to be her two sons, making a difference in their lives and futures.

Dreaming big is an individual pursuit that can lead each of us in various directions, and the rewards are relative to the path that your heart leads you down. What's important is to embrace your story, your path, your heart's desire, and make it your own—living your dream fully and with your whole being.

> Happiness is a very personal feeling, and it's nobody's right to declare what it means to you. And most importantly, happiness is impossible if you're not willing to chase it.
>
> *Cara Alwill Leyba*

When I was an interior designer, I paused to take a real look at my career and where I was heading at the time. I liked the work, but something was missing. More often than not, I wasn't feeling passion in my work. I came to realize that I loved the creativity and communication parts of the job. I would get an incredible high from presenting the big concepts to my clients, helping them expand their vision of possibilities, and creating something that brought joy to their lives. Where it all fell apart for me was in the execution; I didn't enjoy having to then implement the plan, which is of course a critical step to the process if you're offering interior design services! But it wasn't where my talents lay. Once I had designed and established the vision, I was done and wanted to move on to the next creative challenge.

Once I learned about dreaming big, I was able to identify what it was that I loved about my career, and what it was that I didn't enjoy. Once I got clear on the parts that gave me pure joy, I was able to discover a way to evolve my entire company to focus on the parts that I loved. Thus, I created my dream job, one in which I felt doubly enriched, because as an unexpected bonus for doing what I love, I also started to have much greater financial success. This was the beginning of a major evolution for me.

I am drawn toward house and home. Home fulfills and grounds me at a deep emotional level. In fact, my favorite pastime is moving accessories around in my home. It relaxes me. I truly believe that your best life has the potential to begin right in your home. One thing that I knew for sure—the one thing I had no need to question—was that I was in the right industry for myself. I feel at home in the home arena. Once I identified that I loved the creativity and communication parts of my job, I looked for clues in others who were in the home space but weren't overseeing the day-to-day tactical aspects of interior design.

It hit me that Martha Stewart was doing just that. She was communicating a creative vision to others that they in turn implemented in their own homes. She wasn't pulling off the execution for them. The mere idea of this thrilled me. Now mind you, way back then there was a massive divide between what Martha was doing and what I was doing, and I had no clue how I would ever achieve it . . . but I was expanding my vision of possibilities and dreaming big, so at that point the how didn't matter. I had finally identified something that brought me huge excitement. I felt inspired! I then took the time to break it down, asking myself, *What does that inspiration really mean to me?* One of the possibilities that came up for me was, *What if I could communicate DIY design ideas to a larger audience, giving them tools to improve their home environments all on their own, so they wouldn't need to hire a designer at all!* That idea sparked my brainstorming.

Then another idea came: *What if I could create products to help everyone easily establish a well-furnished, comfortable, effortlessly styled home?* Now my head was going a million miles a minute just dreaming up all the possibilities. Keep in mind, this was years before I was hired by HGTV, and I would have never dreamt that I could then move on to an eight-season run as the on-air designer for *The Better Show*. It was long before I wrote any type of magazine or newspaper articles, or authored any books. And back then I had zero knowledge of product development, and a home furnishings company wasn't even a blip on my radar. I still had no idea how I would get to where I wanted to be, but if I hadn't started down the path of expanding my vision, none of this would have ever happened. I was still just dreaming big, but it was all so amazing! I was finally discovering what fulfilled and exhilarated me! Eventually I set small, manageable steps to chart my course—I'll walk you through that part in chapter 5, "The Power of Intentions and Stepping-Stones."

POWER MOVE

Tap into your intuition and your heart and ask yourself: What parts of my current life, job, or hobbies give me great joy? We all know deep down what brings us joy and what does not. If you're feeling hesitant to admit what you like and don't like, be bold and do it anyway! This can be a terrific starting point to identifying your big dream.

As you're identifying what dreaming big means to you, it's normal to experience feelings of doubt, fear, and guilt. Take note of the feelings but try to let them go, so they don't become a stumbling block in your process of identifying what brings you joy in life. Guilt can be particularly troublesome, especially for working mothers who are trying to balance their family lives and careers.

One of the questions I am most frequently asked when I talk to women about dreaming big is, *How do you dream big and still be a good mom to your kids?* If you have a dream of raising a thriving family while simultaneously advancing your career or pursuing some other major life dream, feelings of guilt are common. Guilt can cause you to question whether you're doing your family a disservice by having multiple big dreams, and to wonder if you should hide all the other dreams away while you're raising your kids.

To address this, I felt it important to go right to the source, so I've spent time interviewing several mature "power moms," as I like to call them. These are moms who have set a great example of what many see as "having it all": a flourishing family, along with their pursuit of the other big dreams they have.

Let me introduce you to one of these power moms, Ginnie Roeglin, who is a role model for learning to harness the feelings of mom guilt. Ginnie has two wonderful daughters and a loving marriage of thirty-nine years, plus an extraordinary career that has brought her immense satisfaction. One thing Ginnie knows for sure is that mom guilt can be paralyzing at times . . . if you let it!

Having lived through it personally, the guilt can be debilitating, and moms especially can tend to carry around a lot of guilt. It's unhealthy, stressful, and downright unproductive. No one feels any better because you're feeling guilty. When you feel it, you have to force yourself to let it go. Don't even allow your brain to go there. You have to remind yourself that not every day is going to be in perfect balance. It's about the quality, not the quantity of time, starting with being 100 percent present wherever you are. That said, constantly feeling out of balance and guilty may be about something more than lack of time. You tend to feel balanced when your work aligns with your core values and you feel good about being there.[7]

40

Ginnie started working at age sixteen in the bakery department of a grocery store, slicing loaves of bread and bagging bakery items for customers. Then she moved on to the deli department, slicing meats and packaging salads and other deli items. As she continued through life, she progressed from administrative assistant to marketing assistant to project manager to manager, and then ultimately landed a director position at Costco, one of the largest retailers in the world. And she did all of this while raising two daughters. At the time of our interview, Ginnie had worked for nearly thirty years as an executive with Costco. As senior vice president of e-commerce, travel, and publishing, she oversaw roughly $5 billion in annual revenue. Her job was demanding, yet she absolutely loved it! In addition to her regular job responsibilities, she also fulfilled another major dream by simultaneously serving as chair of the Costco Women's Resource Group, helping other women within Costco achieve their dreams. While doing so added more to her plate, it gave her so much joy to mentor other women in similar situations to hers at an earlier time.

Ginnie not only overcame her own feelings of guilt but has also helped many other moms work through what it means to identify fear and guilt without allowing it to become a self-sabotaging behavior. Even though her own feelings of guilt never went away completely, she was able to intentionally acknowledge the feelings, and then just as intentionally, release them. Ginnie recognized that her feelings were normal, were to be expected, but ultimately it was her choice with what she did with them. She set her intention to have a fulfilling family life and a career, and to continue to move forward despite the feelings of guilt. So Ginnie used this experience to better understand the concerns of other moms and relates to their situations:

> Many people in their late thirties or forties feel trapped, stuck in the life they have ended up in, and believe they can't take a chance because their family is dependent on their income. . . .What happens if they lose their job? Can they afford the time and money it takes to go back to school if necessary? Taking a risk can be difficult. Taking a risk when you have so much riding on it is even harder, but can be entirely worth it.
>
> I certainly had a few setbacks along the way. I came home in tears a few times, too, but I learned a good lesson from every setback and did a little better the next time. Those experiences made me stronger and helped me to build resilience.[8]

Even though it was challenging at times, Ginnie did not let fear get in the way of a fulfilled life, and her family benefited from it. She gave this advice:

> Making sure your work aligns with your core values and beliefs is critical. You also have to feel valued in your job. If you don't, nothing will make you feel balanced. Especially for women, a sense of value is typically even more important than the money. If it's all aligned you'll feel happy even through your busiest times, but if this is lacking you will, without a doubt, feel unhappy and out of balance. If someone feels like they're in that stage of life, it's exhausting—no

question about it—and stressful. If you're in a job that makes you feel trapped, you *have* to do something about it for your own good and for your family's good.[9]

If any of these feelings resonate with you, take a big inhale, and then let it out. Repeat if necessary. Know you are normal and these feelings are to be expected. It's what you do with them that makes all the difference. Guilt can sabotage the potential of your most fulfilled life. If you aren't feeling fulfillment in any area of your life, you must do something about it. Acknowledge the feelings and know that you will be your best for your family when you feel whole and complete. You deserve to have big aspirations, in all aspects of your life, just as much as anyone else.

POWER MOVE

For a moment, give yourself permission to dream with reckless abandon, just like your five-year-old self would have dreamt long before you had any preconceived notions about yourself. Long before anyone told you that you weren't good enough. For a moment, dream like a young, pure, optimistic child.

To help inspire you and to give yourself permission to dream big, ask yourself these questions:

- *What are my deepest desires?*

- *What feelings do I want to experience in my life?*

- *How do I want to spend my time?*

- *If I could have the exact life I want, what would I want out of my relationships, both romantic and otherwise?*

- *What would I choose as my career? Would I even have a career, or is my true desire to be a full-time mom or dad?*

- *If I could live anywhere in the entire world, with nothing holding me back, where would that be?*

- *What experiences would I like to have in my life?*

- *Would I travel more? If so, where do I want to go?*

Susan Feldman is another great role model who had a big dream burning inside of her and went for it despite fear and doubt. Susan is the creator and cofounder of the popular online destination for home furnishings, One Kings Lane.

Susan was inspired to create One Kings Lane after she moved from an apartment in New York City to a house in Los Angeles and experienced the highly fragmented, difficult-to-shop home furnishings industry. An idea was born. Susan joined forces with Alison Pincus, who became her partner, and the two women conceptualized their business model in 2008 during the depths of the US financial and economic crisis. Less than six months later—totally bootstrapping the operation—One Kings Lane launched in March 2009. Today the site is a daily source of shopping and design inspiration for One Kings Lane's avid shoppers.

Susan (along with her business partner) sold One Kings Lane to Bed Bath & Beyond in June 2016. She has been featured in national publications, such as *Elle Decor*, *House Beautiful*, *InStyle*, *New York* Magazine, *Businessweek*, and the *New York Times*. She has appeared on Bravo's *Million Dollar Decorators* and NBC's *The Today Show*. Susan was named in *Vanity Fair*'s New Establishment lists in 2012 and 2013. None of this would have happened had she not dreamed big!

I asked Susan what gave her the drive to go after such an ambitious goal. She replied:

I worked for over twenty years in the fashion business heading up sales and marketing teams for Ralph Lauren Swimwear, Polo Jeans, Warnaco/Authentic Fitness Corp., and Liz Claiborne. The business changed dramatically over the years, and I realized that I was no longer having fun, and definitely wasn't fulfilled. I was at a major crossroads. Should I retire, or go for it and reinvent myself? Reinvention was the winner.

I had an idea that I had been thinking about for at least a year, but I kept questioning if it would work and was the timing right. It didn't help that it was 2008 and it was the worst economic time in history. But I couldn't get this idea out of my mind and I just kept talking about it. One day, my husband said, "Either go do it or please stop talking about it!" . . . It was just what I needed. I jumped . . . well, it felt more like he pushed me in the pool! As soon as I made the decision to go for it the fear went away! The fear I felt that was building bigger and bigger in my head suddenly turned to inspiration and invigoration. I have never had so much fun in my life as when I finally went after my dream![10]

Writing Your Dreams Down

Now is the time, as you begin to give yourself permission, to identify your big dreams by taking the action of putting them down on paper. Why is getting your dreams out of your head and into written form so important? Left in your head, they will swirl around and feel overwhelming or may as well be forgotten. You can write them down in a journal or diary, or you can type them electronically using a program of your choice. (My personal method for capturing my dreams is by using a PowerPoint or Keynote type of electronic document.)

Whatever method you choose to capture your dreams, the emphasis is to be sure to get your dreams and goals out of your head and into a written form that is accessible to you at all times. This isn't something you will create and shelve till next year. This will be your bible, if you will, and it's not to be left behind. It should be at your side at all times. Plus you will be adding to this document as you progress through this book.

POWER MOVE

Once you have your journal or writing program at hand, it's time to ask yourself: If I knew all I had was pure potential, what would I want in life?

As you think about the question above and write your answer, try to get as specific as you can right now. For example: What do you envision for your financial picture? How much money do you want to make, and how much do you want to have saved? Give yourself real dollar amounts. If you want to run a marathon, which one, and how soon?

Take a moment to consider each of the following specific life areas, and add any relevant areas not listed here. Choose one or two that are most important to you at this time, or if you'd rather, tackle the whole thing at once. Write down what you dream of—without any restrictions. This Dream Big List is an exercise in releasing all your limiting beliefs and embracing your pure potential, so dream big!

Career	Residence
Love	Family
Finances	Community
Friendships	Hobbies
Adventure	Health
Travel	Fitness

It's all right if you didn't instantly know the answers to these questions. It's common, actually, because most of us haven't allowed ourselves the privilege of dreaming big. We go through the motions of life, possibly desiring more than our current situation but not knowing what that more would look like, and not feeling inspired by anything specific.

Instead it's easier to remain stagnant, to put off exploring what a more fulfilling life would look like, to wait for another day. And then to make matters worse, if we do have dreams, most of us do not allow ourselves to dream *big*. We automatically impose restrictions and limitations. We worry about what a family member or friend would think. We allow others' opinions and expectations to dominate, which is a self-sabotaging behavior. The sooner you nip this behavior in the bud, the better.

What brings a smile to your face just thinking about it? Whatever that is, that's what you should do more of.

If you're struggling to get clear on what it is you want, one tip is to try something new. There are possibilities all around you if you pay attention. Be curious! Expand your vision. Look at the world with a sense of wonderment. Check out a new city. Look at magazines or read the business section of the newspaper. Find new books that could broaden your interests. Take a yoga class, or meditate to try to still your mind so the ideas start to flow. What brings a smile to your face just thinking about it? Whatever that is, that's what you should do more of.

I learned so much about what I wanted—and did not want—by observing and asking questions of other people who were living happy, fulfilled lives of abundance. It gave me great insight into the different paths that were possible in life. I have always been inquisitive. About everything. My mom tells a funny story of when I was a young child. I was forever asking, "What's that?" over and over again, to the point that one day she could take it no more and stopped right in the middle of the street, threw her hands up in the air, and said, "It's the world!"

This level of curiosity has undoubtedly helped me expand my vision to see all the possibilities that are out there, but it wasn't until I gave myself permission to act on the possibilities that the magic happened. One thing I cannot emphasize enough: if you're not yet clear on the path that is right for you, it's important to stay curious throughout your dreaming process, open your eyes to all possibilities, and ask questions.

Candidly speaking, after going through this process, when friends tell me they still aren't quite sure what they want, every single time, I find they really do know deep down inside, but they are so afraid to say it out loud for fear of what someone might think. Does this resonate with you on any level? If so, acknowledge this dream inside yourself. You don't need to tell anyone about it just yet, but do write it down.

I've been practicing the art of dreaming big for years now, but when I'm not paying attention I can still find myself slipping back into old habits and limiting behaviors, thinking *I wish I could do this*, or *I wish I could do that*, but not realizing that I actually can! Whether it is a lack of time, lack of education, lack of money, or who knows what I come up with as a reason to doubt, when I catch myself doing this, it helps to stop and check in: *Am I just saying I wish I could do this specific thing, or do I really mean it? Is it something I truly desire?* If it is something I truly desire, then the next question is: *Well then, why not me?*

We are all equally deserving of a fulfilled life. What makes one person any more deserving of an experience or a life path than anyone else? The difference is that at some point in life, the person who is fulfilled made the choice to dream, and then also made the choice to take the steps needed to actualize it, turning it into reality.

Dr. Connie Mariano, who ultimately became the lead doctor at the White House for three US presidents, is an extraordinary example of going after the life of her dreams despite seeming to having the odds stacked against her. When she was just two years old, her family immigrated from the Philippines to the United States, where her father joined the US Navy. Her parents had difficulty with communication and with adjusting to the culture, so at a young age she had to be the communicator and the protector of their family. They lived in naval housing on Pearl Harbor, and any spare cash was sent back to the Philippines to take care of their extended family (her father had thirteen siblings). Although they always had food on their plates, life was a struggle, especially for Connie. She tells the story of a pivotal moment:

> My sister was two years old and I was five when we lived in the naval housing in Pearl Harbor, Hawaii. A visiting aunt had let my sister out of her playpen and left her unattended. My sister toddled off into the backyard and the adjoining

parking lot where my father was waxing the car. The phone rang and my father put down the canister of liquid wax onto the pavement as he ran into the house to answer the phone. My sister saw the shiny canister, and thinking it was a drink, took a swig of the liquid wax.

I found her on the pavement, unconscious, and I knew, even though I was only five years old, that there was something wrong with her. I called my parents, who ran over as my sister had a seizure. The scene became chaotic as my parents grabbed my sister, four-year-old brother, and me, jumped into our car, and dashed off to Tripler Army Hospital up the hill from where we lived.

I accompanied my mother and my unconscious sister into the exam room to see the doctor. My father, guilt-ridden, sat in the waiting room holding my brother. My mother avoided eye contact with the doctor as he tried to get a history. In the midst of his examination of my sister, she had a second seizure. At that point, the doctor said out loud, "Oh, your daughter has epilepsy!"

I knew that was not correct. My mother, who still had not adjusted to the culture and had language barriers, was too ashamed and intimidated to question the doctor and instead was silent and acquiescent. Noting her silence, I piped up, "Mommy, tell the doctor that the baby drank the poison!"

The doctor heard me and questioned my mother, "Is that true? Did the baby drink poison? What type?"

My mother had the empty canister in her purse and took it out and showed the doctor. The doctor looked at the contents of the canister and said, "We need to pump the baby's stomach and put her in intensive care, now!"

My sister survived her week in the hospital and had no adverse effects (or memory) of what happened. But what was lost was my confidence that my parents had the tools to take care of us and set us on a meaningful path for our futures. At the young age of five, I knew that I had to rely upon myself.[11]

After that Connie and her family moved from place to place, wherever her father was stationed. They were living in Taipei, Taiwan, when, at fourteen, Connie took part in a career day in her school. An OB-GYN stopped by and talked about what it was like to deliver babies, and that's when a spark went off in Connie. She remembered how her paternal grandmother had died at thirty-four while giving birth to her eighth child in a hut on a remote island of the Philippines. In that career day moment, Connie knew that she wanted to become a doctor and make sure this didn't happen to anyone ever again. She had no idea how she was going to become an OB-GYN, but the dream stayed with her. After years of determination and hard work, a path opened up—a path that eventually took her all the way to the White House!

No matter where your background has brought you to today, you, too, can have a path open up that can lead to your most fulfilled life. You must first identify what you want and love from your core. And even though the how-to isn't clear yet, don't let that stop you from exploring your biggest, boldest dreams!

POWER MOVE

Remember that at this point you do not need to know how you will pull off your dreams; that shouldn't factor in at all yet. The point is to expand your vision. Read through each of your dreams one more time. With each dream, ask yourself:

- *Is this honestly what I want, or did I subconsciously put a restriction on myself when writing this down?*

- *Is there someone talking in my ear, saying* You should *or* You shouldn't *as I write down my dream? If so, I will try hard to shut out that voice and write down what I want.*

- *Deep inside, do I want an even more elevated version of this dream?*

The Spark of Desire

Desire itself can be weighed down by a negative connotations— you might be afraid that you're being selfish or that you're doing something wrong if you "give in" to your desires. Deepak Chopra sheds light on this misconception by describing how a deep desire is not selfish, but a divine wish, a divine seed connecting us to our true destinies.

Exploring your desires, your dreams, is an inspiring process. And inspiration is a driving motivator in all areas of life.

Dream so big it almost scares you.

It's even okay if you start to experience feelings of guilt or fear for dreaming so big. Dream so big it almost scares you. Possibly this is the first time you've ever given yourself permission to let go, and at first it feels uncomfortable. Remember the example Ginnie Roeglin shared with us earlier in this chapter. It's normal to feel guilt sometimes. Just let the feelings in and then let them pass. We will spend a good portion of this book learning to identify the fear and using it to propel us forward. For now, just feel it and let it go. Hopefully, though, you're starting to be filled with excitement, and a glimmer of hope for a more fulfilled life.

There is no passion to be found playing small—in settling for a life that is less than the one you are capable of living.
Nelson Mandela

The beauty of the exercise of dreaming big, without restrictions, is that you can keep the process going forever. Whatever you wrote down throughout this chapter can change, as you will undoubtedly continue to evolve. And remember, you still don't need to know how you will get there.

POWER MOVE

I continually reexamine my goals and dreams. In fact, I make a habit of doing it every January 1 and every year on my birthday, as these dates are inspiring to me. On these days I revisit and rewrite my goals as needed. This forces me to make sure that I still like the path I'm on and that I'm not just doing it out of habit. This process refreshes me every time I do it!

THE POWER OF
YOUR MIND

*Whether you believe you can do a thing
or not, you are right.*
Henry Ford

One power you possess right now—in fact, you've had it all along—is your mind. I can't emphasize how important, how downright crucial your mind-set is to experiencing a fulfilling life. Your mind is incredibly valuable, and it can be used for the betterment or the detriment of your life. Your mind-set is up to you.

Whether you've opted to manage it well, or you've opted not to manage it at all, you can reclaim control over your mind at the very moment you decide to take ownership. Anthony Robbins says, "Whatever you hold in your mind on a consistent basis is exactly what you will experience in your life."[12] This has proven true for me more times than I can tell you, and you can experience it too.

Thomas Edison "failed" many times in his life but kept driving forward. In 1869, he saw inefficiency in the way Congress voted, so he patented an electric vote recorder system. When he presented his new device to the senators, they dismissed it. What to Edison was an unnecessarily slow voting process was to the senators a desirable pace, one in tune with political traditions and procedures. They didn't want or need a new vote-tally system. Instead of throwing in the towel, Edison realized that he had misjudged his audience, and he vowed that from then on he would work on only inventing things that people wanted.[13]

After beginning to find some commercial success in the following years, Edison decided to strive for a grand achievement, an electric light that was practical and economical, not to mention safe for consumers. It took several years and thousands of iterations of his designs, but finally he created the electric industry and laid the framework for the electric age we all benefit from today. About this herculean task, we've heard these famous words attributed to Edison: "I have not failed. I have just found 10,000 ways that won't work." He believed in himself and his idea and knew that all he needed was one more idea. His positive mind-set did not leave room for doubt or a sense of failure.

With some simple practices, you can bring about a shift in your mind-set, which will undoubtedly move you forward to your most fulfilled life. These practices can be applied to everything from a business meeting to a major life goal, and they don't require a lot of time. You don't need to buy anything, go anywhere, or even take notes; it's all work that you do in your head!

Mental visualization can actually help decrease any worry you are carrying around.

Visualization

In the next chapters we will discuss setting intentions and creating vision boards, which are two powerful tools that have helped dreams come true for millions and millions of people. However, there's an even older, more widely practiced form of visualization that, when used in combination with vision boards, helps launch your intentions forward. It's a mental visualization technique where you play out a scenario in your head, from beginning to end, before it has actually occurred. You might now be saying to yourself, *Oh, I recognize that, it's called worry!* No, my friend, that's not what we're talking about here. Mental visualization can actually help decrease any worry you are carrying around. Because when you play out your dream situation in your mind, see your desired result, and then practice the exercise over and over again, you strengthen your ability to fully embody and realize your dream.

Research has shown that "mental practices are almost [as] effective as true physical practice, and that doing both is more effective than either alone. . . . Brain studies now reveal that thoughts produce the same mental instructions as actions. . . . The brain is getting trained for actual performance during visualization."[14]

Professional athletes have been using this powerful visualization tool for years to achieve success. Olympic gold medalist skier Lindsey Vonn had this to share: "I always visualize the run before I do it. . . . Once I visualize a course, I never forget it. So I get on those lines and go through exactly the run that I want to have."[15]

Many golfers also use mental visualization before every shot. They envision the flight path and the ball landing exactly how and where they want it to land. Before getting to the course, they may visualize the entire golf course, playing it out shot by shot in their minds. Widely deemed the greatest golfer of all time, Jack Nicklaus has said: "I never hit a shot, not even in practice, without having a very sharp, in-focus picture of it in my head."[16]

World-class athletes find that visualization dramatically aids their performance. We, too, can use our minds to visualize our "game" and set our intentions to bring about desired results.

POWER MOVE

Pick one of your biggest dreams. Let it play out in your mind—visualize it scene by scene, from start to successful finish.

For example, if you are hoping to land a new dream job, imagine you have received the phone call for an interview.

- *Walk yourself visually through the whole experience, from getting dressed to arriving at the interview.*

- *Visualize walking into the office, smiling, and shaking hands.*

- *Imagine the conversation and interview questions, as well as the confidence of your answers.*

- *Picture it through to the end of the interview, to the positive energy expressed as you say good-bye.*

- *Keep going with the visualization: imagine receiving the phone call telling you that you landed the job! The competition was fierce, yet you nailed it and now it is yours! See and feel the success.*

Replay that visualization in slow motion and reflect on it through all your senses. Where are you in your visualization? Picture the environment in your mind. Create it as clearly as possible and with as much detail as you can. Imagine yourself in that environment, living out the achievement of your dream:

- *Feel the environment through your sense of touch. Is the sun hitting your face? Are you holding someone's hand? Is there a warm breeze?*

- *Hear the sounds that surround you. Are birds chirping? Are waves crashing on a beach? Is there a background hum of conversation or traffic?*

- *Smell the scent of your environment. What aromas are around you? A delicious dinner? Freshly cut grass?*

- *Taste the flavors in your environment. Are you holding a drink in your hand? What is it? Freshly brewed coffee? Maybe a glass of wine? Or are you taking a bite of that delicious dinner?*

- *Experience the emotions of your environment. Using your sixth sense, your intuition, how does this all feel to you? Allow it to wash over you. Let it all in. Feel the flood of emotions that well up.*

Is there a smile on your face? I hope so! Acknowledge that. Are tears of joy trailing down your cheeks? Are you jumping up and down with excitement? Who are you going to call first? Your mom? Your partner or best friend? Hear the thrill in your voice, and say the words in your mind exactly as you would tell your closest friend. What is your mind saying? *I did it! I got it! I am SO excited, I can hardly stand it! Let's celebrate!*

Be your dream; see it constantly and envision the exact outcome you want—over and over and over again.

You have just created your personal life movie. It's a movie written about your biggest dream, and you just watched it come true! You are the star of this movie, and you control every scene. This is your very own power tool. Use it! At a minimum, do this visualization at least twice a week. When you can see the outcome in your mind, you are also sending positive energy into the world, and you can make it your reality. Remember the power of attraction: like attracts like. Be your dream; see it constantly and envision the exact outcome you want—over and over and over again.

You can also try this with something as routine as a phone conversation or a business meeting. It's so easy to fret that a conversation, a meeting, or a pitch won't go your way. Instead of spending time agonizing over what could go wrong, take control of your mind by shifting your mind-set and letting go of worries. Visualizing the outcome you want can do wonders.

POWER MOVE

Before entering into a conversation or meeting, visualize the way you want the situation to go. See the desired outcome in your mind. Play it over and over again until you truly embody it.

For example:

- *Visualize the whole situation from the moment you walk into the space: your handshake, the moment when your eyes and smiles first meet, the warmth exchanged between you.*

- *See yourself as you sit down and the words just flow. Laughter and lighthearted conversation come easy for both of you today. There's a mutual respect established, and the person you're meeting with loves your ideas! They offer up some constructive feedback, and that's great! They're engaging with you and giving you hints as to how you can get a yes!*

- *And in the end, see yourself getting exactly what you set out to get from this meeting.*

Get in the habit of paying attention to your thoughts before every conversation and every meeting—every situation you care about. If you are dedicated to imagining only positive outcomes, and you don't let even a shadow of doubt or negativity cross your mind, you will experience a transformation in your typical outcomes.

If you have a habit of coming home and running for the chip bag, try visualizing a different pattern on your drive home. Take a deep breath and imagine how you would like your evening to go.

Embrace the food that nourishes you. All of it. And let the junk go. It's one way to take ownership of your limiting patterns and change them. It makes a huge difference!

Visualization even works with personal relationships. Play a visual movie in your mind before you engage in a conversation that could be emotionally charged. What this does is put you in the driver's seat. You are taking responsibility for the only thing you can control: your actions and behaviors. Again, remember that like attracts like. Be the person you want to have reflected back to you in your movie before you enter into the conversation. Trust me, the effect will be disarming when you show up to the conversation with a totally different energy than the other person is expecting.

Positive Thinking

One morning while I was having breakfast out, a golf interview was on the TV in the restaurant. The golfer being interviewed was discussing why he didn't win the tournament. He chalked it all up to the lack of a positive mind-set! He said he couldn't shake his negative attitude after hitting a bad shot out of the bunker. How powerful is that?

A positive mind-set plays a big part in actualizing your goals and intentions. How often have you seen people who have had a significant measure of success in their lives walk around with the glass half-empty? It's typically the opposite. Meet someone who has actualized their deepest desires in life and they usually, if not always, see the glass half-full.

If you're anything like me, a positive mind-set is most difficult when we're around those who are closest to us. My husband often becomes the dumping ground for everything that has challenged me throughout my day. I easily tell the positive to everyone else, and just as easily share the negative with him. That doesn't do anything good for our relationship. When I catch myself in the act and make a conscious effort to reflect positivity—especially with those who are closest to me—it changes my relationships for the better.

You're already thinking during every second of every day, so you might as well think positively!

Mind-set is a choice. With just an attitude shift in the way you view yourself and your situations, you can create major change in your life. It doesn't take any extra time out of your already busy schedule. You're already thinking during every second of every day, so you might as well think positively! The payback is immense, and it energizes and enhances our overall well-being, decision making, and resilience. Positive psychologist and author Martin Seligman has this insight to share from his book *Authentic Happiness*: "A positive mood . . . buoys people into a way of thinking that is creative, tolerant, constructive, generous, undefensive and lateral. This way of thinking aims to detect not what is wrong, but what is right."[17]

Do you see the glass half-full or half-empty? Either way you view it, it is a choice you are making. Choose to view the glass half-full every time. It's so easy to slip into negative thinking, which is counterproductive to letting your dreams flow into your life. Negativity breeds more negativity. No one positive wants to be around someone negative. It just sucks the life out of the room and the energy out of the conversation. But everyone wants to be around someone positive. You will attract positive people who will support your most fulfilled life when you own a positive mind-set. Try to find the good in each situation.

"The positive emotions of confidence,
hope, and trust, for example,
serve us best not when life is easy,
but when life is difficult."
Martin E.P. Seligman, PhD, *Authentic Happiness*

My mom comes to mind when I think about positivity. No matter what might be going on around her she always maintains a positive outlook. The other day I was in an airport on my way to a speaking engagement, feeling overly tired and nervous, when I got a call from my Mom, all the way from Africa. As we were talking, I noticed her voice was more quiet than usual. I asked her if she was OK, and she hesitantly told me about a very severe illness she was experiencing. In shock and worry I gasped, "Mom, why didn't you say anything?!" And she immediately replied, "Because this will pass, and I am having so many great experiences in my life that I don't want to waste my time talking to you about the negative." That immediately shifted my focus back to the gratitude of what was going on in my life. It lifted any feelings of being tired, and changed my nervousness into excitement. Just a subtle shift in my perception and my entire day felt joyful.

POWER MOVE

Choose a positive mind-set. Catch yourself the moment negativity about a person or a situation starts to take hold. Do not allow it to stay. Always view yourself as a success! Only you have the power to shift your thinking, and you will attract more of the positive when you, yourself, are positive.

Gratitude is the quickest disruptor of a bad mood.

The Ultimate Disruptor

Want a simple trick to get yourself from negative to positive thinking? Practice gratitude. Gratitude is the quickest disruptor of a bad mood. Find something to be grateful for, even if it's something simple, and you will soon find yourself smiling. It's hard to be grateful and negative at the same time. Try it! I bet you can't think of something that makes you grateful and not smile at the same time.

Gratitude shifts your mind-set to the positive. So how do you get into the habit of using gratitude as a tool? Practicing gratitude is like exercising a muscle; through repetition you can get it to be second nature, like muscle memory, if you will.

When I first started dating my husband, we had a long-distance relationship. Every time we would meet up, no matter where we were, he had a white notebook with him. First thing in the morning, even before brushing his teeth, he would sit on the edge of the tub and write down five things he was grateful for. He didn't miss a single morning. He swore it changed the outcome of even the most challenging of days, by starting off with a grateful mind-set. He no longer needs his notebook, since he says gratitude now comes easily to him.

Inspired by my husband, but with a twist, I made myself get into a habit of writing down five things I'm grateful for before I go to bed. And when I say made myself, I mean it. Typically the last thing I want to do when I'm tired is think more, but the reason I find nighttime gratitude so effective in shifting my mind-set is that it forces me to look for moments of gratitude all day long. When evening comes, my gratitude list requires little thought because I've been aware of grateful moments throughout my day, thus feeling happier and more positive overall, even during tough times.

You can find gratitude in unexpected places, and that's what makes it so amazing. Say you have a coworker who drives you crazy. When you're forced to look for moments of gratitude throughout your day, you can switch the frustration you might otherwise feel to empathy by appreciating your colleague for who she is at heart and acknowledging the challenges she is facing. Gratitude is a mind-set and a choice, but it can become a way of life.

Say thank you even for small acts. Even if it means thanking someone for something they're supposed to do or are being paid to do. Showing appreciation makes you feel good, and it makes them feel good too. Gratitude is contagious. As you begin using gratitude as a tool, be prepared for more of the good stuff to continually flow into your life!

POWER MOVE

Go to gratitude when you need a pick-me-up. If this doesn't come naturally for you, pick a time of day and write down at least five things you're grateful for. Try it for just eleven days, and see what happens! I bet you'll start seeing your world in a whole new light.

Decluttering Your Mind

Too often we allow clutter to accumulate in our lives, both physically and mentally. Clutter and incomplete projects take up space in the valuable real estate of our minds. Things left undone can bring about feelings of guilt, negativity, and stress, which are mental distractions that can make you feel bad about yourself. You might feel unworthy of accomplishing something big in life when you can't ever seem to complete the small things.

Jack Canfield offers a great perspective into this from his book *The Success Principles*:

Like incompletes, daily irritants are equally damaging to your success because they, too, take up attention units. Perhaps it's the missing button on your favorite suit that keeps you from wearing it to an important meeting or the torn screen on your patio door that lets in annoying insects. One of the best things you can do to move further and faster along your success path is to fix, replace, mend, or get rid of those daily irritants that annoy you and stay on your mind.[18]

POWER MOVE

These are a few of my favorite tips on decluttering and finishing incompletes:

- Make a list of all the incomplete projects in your life, around your home, and even at your office. Drawers you need to organize, areas you need to clean up, or things you need to get rid of that no longer serve for you. Try to think of everything.

- Once you have your list of incompletes, prioritize them. You don't have to tackle these all at once; in fact, trying to do that would most likely be setting yourself up for failure. Put the most pressing project at the top of the list, or the one that causes you the most distress.

- Break each item on your list into small stepping-stones. Doing so makes projects appear much more manageable.

- Give yourself a timeline for completion, and put it on your calendar.

If you can only afford five minutes a day—and it could take a full week to tackle one thing—that's okay. As with your larger life goals, get yourself in the habit of writing down your messes and incompletes, and then breaking them into stepping-stones, or bite-size pieces, with bite-size time frames before adding manageable deadlines to your calendar.

You've just created your stepping-stones to experiencing a decluttered life, thus creating space for the good to flow more freely. You've taken your big projects and broken them down into manageable pieces, and you will soon be doing this for your life intentions, too. This step works just as effectively for major goals as it does for your minor projects that seem more like nuisances than goals. (If you want to learn more about how to declutter and manage incompletes, I share in-depth information in my book *Love Coming Home*.)

Quieting the Mind

Hand in hand with decluttering your mind is quieting your mind in order to optimize its powers, as well as open up space for the good. When I'm feeling in a rut and can't get to that positive mind-set I need to continue progressing toward my dreams, I know it's time to pause, relax, and quiet my mind.

A quiet mind opens you up to possibilities, and it's an easy way to regain your positive power.

Your mind is powerful, and it can at times go into overdrive, necessitating a complete reset. Quieting your mind might sound counterintuitive to positive thinking, as thinking is, well, thinking. It's a mind activity. However, a quiet mind opens you up to possibilities, and it's an easy way to regain your positive power.

Have you ever noticed you typically solve some of your biggest problems, or have some of your most creative ideas, in the middle of the night while you are sleeping? When your mind is at a state of rest some of your biggest breakthroughs occur. This is most definitely how it is for me. My mind works its best when it is at rest. There are many ways to quiet your mind. I have two personal favorites that have worked effectively for me for years: meditation and yoga. They're like a secret power to use anytime I need a mental reset or clarity. And they don't have to be lengthy exercises or long mindfulness sessions to make a big impact.

In his book *Getting in the Gap*, Dr. Wayne Dyer says:

Think of thoughts as things, which need silence between them to attract and manifest new forms into life. Two bricks can't be fastened together to form a wall without a space for mortar. The mortar itself is comprised of particles, which require spaces to allow them to become mortar. Our thoughts are the same. They require a pause between them to give life to what they represent separately. This is the gap, and it's a space that allows us to build, create, imagine, and manifest all that we're capable of creating with those thoughts.[19]

One misconception about meditation is that it has to be done perfectly. Another is that it takes lots of skill to sit still that long. Yet another is that you're doing it wrong if you can't keep thoughts from racing in and out of your mind. All of that is wrong. There is no perfect way to meditate. Do what works for you.

The most important part of meditation is that you're comfortable. You can sit upright on a floor pillow or, if you wish, on a chair or sofa to support your back. There is even a form of meditation where you lie on your back with your lower legs up on a chair. That variation feels great. Do what works for you . . . but don't get so comfortable that you fall asleep!

Meditate for as long as you have time for. Even if that's only three minutes! It counts. Some of the meditation apps that I use offer one-minute meditations. The longer you can meditate, the more effective it can become, but you have to be realistic about what fits into your schedule. The beauty of meditation is that you can use it as a quick fix, a feel-good remedy anytime you need it.

If you decide to make meditation a daily practice, which I highly recommend, I find it most effective to pick a time of day that you can consistently commit to. For me, what's working right now is to meditate right when I wake up. I brush my teeth, take my vitamins, and then meditate for ten minutes. The time flies by. Afterward I grab my coffee and get on with my morning.

Those ten minutes could have been wasted online or by futzing around the kitchen, but when I've used that interval for meditation, I feel an incredible difference in my mind-set for the day. I feel so much calmer and more ready to take on the world. Meditation somehow puts everything in life into perspective. Doing something that empowers you also provides a great sense of accomplishment with which to kick-start your day. And it's only been fifteen minutes since you got out of bed!

You might be thinking, *What if my mind is racing?* Mine does every single time! I have high hopes of someday meditating like a monk, but so far, no luck! The key is to acknowledge the thoughts and then let them go. For me, the easiest way to bring myself back to the present in meditation is to focus on my breathing. Pay attention to your breath as it goes in and out of your body. More specifically, I find if I focus my attention on the sensation of breath as it goes in and out of my nostrils, it really goes a long way in keeping me present in my meditation. When you get distracted again, because you will, just go right back to your breath. Continue to repeat that cycle and you will get through your meditation with a surprisingly clear and positive mind-set.

You can practice meditations that are silent, accompanied by music, or even guided by words. I've done quite a bit of research on the topic, as at the beginning I was on the quest for a perfect form of meditation, and I've come to the conclusion that no one form of meditation is the best. To each their own.

I've deeply appreciated the gifts I've received from Oprah and Deepak's series of guided meditations. Each day's meditation comes with a powerful message—one that seems to have been created specifically for me, and to arrive at just the right time. Whether you prefer guided meditations or musical accompaniment, you'll find an abundant variety of apps you can download to your phone or computer. There are even silent meditations that begin with the sound of a harmonious bell and end the same way. You choose the time length you desire and are then free to relax in the quiet. With meditation now mainstream and widely practiced, you have easy access to whatever type of meditation suits you the best at any given moment. Even just meditating in complete silence is great too. That is my typical airplane go-to method.

You can also do walking meditations, during which you are deeply present as you walk. Those are amazing! Something I once heard that really struck me, "You're here, so you might as well be here!" (Great advice for everything in life.) Walking meditations are all about being in the here and now with all of your senses. Walk with a whole new appreciation for what's around you. Notice every sound you can hear. See everything with a fresh set of eyes. Smell every scent around you. Feel your clothes on your skin, the wind on your face, and the pavement or grass beneath your feet. Even let your taste buds come fully alive. What flavors are in your mouth? Take in the world as if you were experiencing it for the first time. Also tap into your sixth sense, your intuition. What is it telling you? It's amazing how a walking meditation quiets the mind. Try it for three minutes or thirty. Any length you choose will be helpful.

Learning how to still my mind is one of the best gifts I've ever received. If you try it even once, you will notice that it brings you right back to what matters most. You will start to see circumstances and people with greater clarity. You will feel happier and more powerful. If your first experience with meditation feels a bit challenging, that's normal and to be expected. It takes practice, which is what meditation is all about, but I encourage you to hang in there. If you do, your meditations will more often than not flow with ease and joy, and you will come to relish them.

> The more man meditates upon good thoughts, the better will be his world and the world at large.
>
> *Confucius*

POWER MOVE

Use whatever calming method you find effective for you, but get in the habit of routinely quieting your mind—ideally for a certain amount of time each day. Give your mind the opportunity to rest and reset.

Meditation has been practiced successfully for centuries, and its benefits are more widely recognized today than ever before. Your mind-set is critical to realizing your most fulfilled life. You can gain control over your mind-set and shift your entire world if you want to! Practice visualization, maintain a positive outlook, make gratitude a habit, and quiet your mind with meditation—these four fundamental tools will make your mind powerful beyond measure!

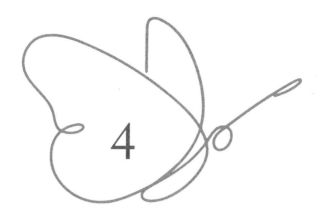

THE POWER OF
VISION BOARDS

Dare to live the life you have dreamed
for yourself. Go forward and make
your dreams come true.
Ralph Waldo Emerson

We all need a little bit of magic in our lives to help us get to our most fulfilled version of ourselves. For me, that magic has been the use of vision boards. Simply put, there is something about putting my goals and intentions on a vision board that make my wildest dreams come true! It even works for my smallest of intentions, both with circumstances and physical objects I desire. A vision board is the spark that helps launch all of the powers in this book.

Through vision boards, you can see your dreams before you. You can then envision yourself in that circumstance, living your dream. It is an extraordinarily powerful act.

As we discussed in chapter 3, mental visualization is an incredibly powerful practice when harnessed, and it's a key to effective goal setting. A vision board is also a potent form of visualization—it uses your visual sense. When layered with your mental practice, it stimulates and optimizes the practice of visualization into an extremely transformational tool.

To put it simply, a vision board is a place for gathering images and phrases that convey the intentions, emotions, feelings, experiences, accomplishments, and possessions you want to have in life—to help you visualize your goals and dreams. It gives you the power to see your life, as you truly want it to be. A vision board helps you focus on what matters most, motivating you to take the needed steps to make that your reality.

Through vision boards, you can see your dreams before you. You can then envision yourself in that circumstance, living your dream. It is an extraordinarily powerful act. To this day I use vision boards for everything: personal goals, business goals, and my home décor goals. I even created a vision board for this book!

As you are creating your vision board, you still don't need to know exactly how you will get there. We'll get into building your path to your dreams in chapter 5, "The Power of Intentions and Stepping-Stones." For now, I want you to continue to expand your awareness of all the possibilities that are out there by creating your personal Dream Big Vision Board.

What are your deepest desires? What makes your heart sing? Where would you like to travel? Where do you want to live? What does your dream home look like? How do you want to feel each day when you wake? How much money do you want to have? Are you seeking a new love relationship? What does that look like to you? Do you want deeper friendships or perhaps an expanded family? What about a pet to love?

The answers to such questions should go right up on your vision board in the form of photos, cutout images, and meaningful phrases. Refer back to your Dream Big List from chapter 2 throughout this process. But also, as you browse for images and snippets of text, I encourage you to be open to new ideas, circumstances, places, and even physical objects that speak to you—things that you haven't thought of before but that inspire you now. This happens quite frequently. The use of photos and clipped images in establishing what you want, on a material level, and especially on a spiritual and circumstantial level, is extremely important. It opens your eyes and mind to potential and possibility.

Once I put everything up on a board together, something magical happened. Suddenly I could see the life I wanted right before my eyes!

The most important part of the process of creating your Dream Big Vision Board is to gather images that evoke positive feelings for *you*, not for anyone else. If this process is too personal at this point, feel free to keep your board private so only you can see it. I'll say more on this a little later in the chapter. For now, stay open and curious. Scour magazines and printed materials of all types to see if anything sparks your interest or makes your heart yearn for that specific situation.

At the same time, also explore images of what you wrote on your Dream Big List in chapter 2. Reflect on these questions as you collect and add your images to your board: When you see the situation, object, or circumstance right in front of you as an image, how does it feel to you? Does it bring a smile to your face? Does the image resonate with you? Try to gather and save images the moment you find them. They are precious, and you might not stumble on an image that makes you feel the same way again.

By the same logic, if you see an image that exemplifies a goal on your Dream Big List, and you get a sudden pang of unease about it, sit with that feeling. Don't ignore it, and don't automatically cut out and save the image. Reflect on why you are feeling that way now. Perhaps your goal has changed or evolved into something else? At this point you haven't wasted any time forcing a life path that isn't meant for you. The feelings you will uncover while looking at images for your board are revealing. Pay attention to them.

Look for images and ideas everywhere. This is a fun process. It brings you to the here and now everywhere you happen to be. When you see something you like, snap a photo of it. It's not only an inspiring activity but calming too. It's almost like a walking meditation. You have to be in the present moment to notice everything around you. Walk around with a keen awareness. Notice the possibilities.

If you see something that creates a spark in you, use that spark as consideration for your board. If there is someone you personally admire in your life, and you have his or her permission, snap a photo for use on your board! Hold off on photographing strangers, though, as that could get awkward. But if you see a place you'd love to live in, or a cause you want to help, snap a photo. Is there a car or a home you'd enjoy owning someday? All of that can go up on your vision board. Your board should be a treasure chest that holds your deepest desires and intentions.

Getting Your Vision Board Started

I am frequently asked if all of the various images should go on separate boards based on topic, or if they should be kept together in one spot. Well, I can tell you what I've learned, as I've tried it both ways. First of all, there is no right or wrong answer. Both are a little bit right. However, through personal trial and error, I have found it much more effective for me to have all of my images in one place. I first tried a page for each dream topic, and I would flip through the images several times a day. That worked for a while, but once I put everything up on a board together, something magical happened. Suddenly I could see the life I wanted right before my eyes! It was all there at a glance, and so harmonious! Seeing everything flowing together inspired great excitement and motivation to turn it into reality.

Seeing all my dream images in one place also brought to light contradicting dreams. For example, there was a time when I thought it would be fun to have a daily TV show like Martha Stewart's, but a good part of my vision board was about freedom and flexibility of schedule. Those two dreams didn't match, and neither did they fit the life I truly wanted, as a daily show with an intense schedule would leave little room for flexibility. I adjusted my TV dream and instead focused on creating entertaining, lifestyle-related content that could inspire others to live their best lives possible, starting at home. As soon as I made that shift in mind-set and reflected it in my images, I was able to see and find a path to make that happen. Ultimately I was offered a biweekly spot on a national TV show that allowed me to share my passion with a broader group of individuals without cramping my schedule. It left me plenty of time to run my business and be with friends and family. There is a lot of power to seeing your images all at a glance on one board!

There was also a time when I experimented with two boards, one for business and one for my personal life, but it started to feel like I was two different people with two different lives and sets of desires. It didn't feel harmonious. I wanted my life to flow seamlessly, not be chopped up into separate parts, living my business life during the day and then going home to live my personal life at night. The feelings and emotions I wanted to experience in life were not meant to be part time. The loving, fun, joyful moments expressed on my personal board were meant to be carried through to my business day, and the sense of accomplishment I felt from my work, I wanted to carry home with me at night. I stopped separating the boards and merged my life back together onto one integrated board. Now I no longer accept business commitments that will contradict the type of personal life I desire, as my board brings my entire being into focus.

If you have only one board, it's easier to keep it with you all the time. Choose the location where you typically spend the most time, and make that your primary board location . . . that is, if privacy is not an issue. Take a photo of your board and tape it onto the wall at your secondary location. Also keep a photo of your board in your phone, in your wallet, and even in your car. Your vision board is a great source of inspiration; you'll want it with you all the time.

Another common question asked of me is what kind of board or format is best. Well, again there's no single answer. You can use a corkboard, poster board, blank wall, closet or bathroom mirror, shoebox, or even the refrigerator door, if you choose. If you prefer a digital format, use a phone app or any program that lets you conveniently capture and save images. Pinterest is a great tool for digital vision boards. (My personal preference is a framed corkboard, but that's just me.)

It's important to place your vision board where you can view the images daily. Seeing it frequently is key to the process. If you want your board to remain private, and you opt to create it electronically, set an alert on your phone to remind you to look at your board at regular intervals.

POWER MOVE

To create your vision board, you need a place to display images and photos—perhaps a framed corkboard or poster, a fabric board, or a large, flat piece of cardboard. That surface or substrate can be hung on your wall or it can be freestanding for mobility. You can also use a photo album or a three-ring binder with transparent pocket pages. Even a shoebox, a refrigerator door, or a bathroom mirror can work.

Create a vision board that is convenient and easy to use, and something that you don't have to permanently fix each image to.

Once you have identified the way in which you will display your images, start to select, cut out, and pin images to your vision board. (You might want to move things around later, so don't get out the superglue!) The images you choose should be ones that evoke the emotions, feelings, circumstances, and situations you desire. Be open to discovering new dreams when you stumble upon a new image that spontaneously expands your vision.

For instance, if you desire romance, choose images that evoke the situations you crave: a loving embrace on the beach, or having wine by a fire with a partner. If you yearn for peace and solitude, possibly you will select an image of a lovely field or forest where you can escape and relax on your own. If you want to bring more money into your life, add the exact amount you want to your vision board—even try writing yourself a blank check dated in the near future, and put it up. You will be delightfully surprised to see what happens.

In my conversation with John Assaraf, author and pioneer in the world of vision boards, he had this to share with me: "When you create a vision board, you concretize what you want through images, giving clarity and direction." I then asked him if he still uses a vision board; he answered, "I use them all the time. I do them with my wife and kids. Now, though, I've come to understand that a vision board needs to be married with action and work, what I call the GOYA principle." Which he went on to explain meant, "Get Off Your Ass and do something about it!"[20]

POWER MOVE

Look for images everywhere. Magazines are readily available. Scour each magazine with fresh eyes; maybe it houses your dreams! Explore the internet for images and words that are significant to you. Snap photos of book pages or other printed materials you'd rather not cut up. And take your camera along when you go for a walk or a drive. You'll notice inspiring images all around once you begin paying attention to them.

As you find the images that speak to you, semi-permanently affix them to your vision board, which is meant to evolve. You may well discover new images that are more inspiring, or want to move a specific dream to another position on the board. Your board never has to be complete. You will continually evolve, and your board is the perfect place to display your current and future desires.

Since your images are semifixed, you get to remove them and file them away as your dreams come true! It's almost like checking something off your to-do list. And best of all, it's uplifting to open a file folder of images that have all come to fruition. This is a major pick-me-up. Hang on to these images; you'll need them someday.

If a certain dream has come true for you and you want to continue to live it each day, keep it on your board. It doesn't ever need to come down. Or if you have something in your life that you currently cherish and want more of it, or simply want to sustain it, keep images of it on your board as long as you want.

For example, if you're in a loving relationship, keep images that represent that love front and center at all times. It's so easy to take the ones we love for granted and slip into negative behaviors. I am the first to admit that I can slip into that mode in no time. However, just one glance at my board, seeing photos of my husband and the love that I dreamed of and now have, quickly gets me back to gratitude and changes my behaviors. These are the kinds of images you may not want to take down and file away. Ever.

When deciding where to keep your vision board, choose a place where you can see it multiple times a day. If at first you want to keep it in your closet, so it's more private, that's okay. As you start to see the magic behind it unfold, you'll more than likely want to move it to a more prominent spot in your home or office, and you won't care who sees it. In fact, you will undoubtedly inspire others to do the same.

When you walk into the conference room of Beyond Words Publishing, who publishes my books and also published *The Secret*, you see staff members' dreams—even the publisher's dreams—prominently placed on vision boards for the entire company to see. It's a concept they live every day! For me, it was incredibly powerful to see the coming together of their entire team for common goals.

> As you continue to grow, evolve and expand, your dreams will too. Your vision board is meant to be kept and cherished. They chronicle not only your dreams, but your growth and achievements.
>
> *Jack Canfield*

Vision boards are fun to create as a family or with friends. Some of the best bonding time can be when doing boards together. You can all pile onto the family room floor together with lots of magazines and plenty of scissors. My cousins and I have done it at Thanksgiving. It elicits the best, most heartfelt conversations. You get to learn a lot about family, friends, or coworkers when working on vision boards together.

Find magazines on a variety of subjects: travel, mindfulness, sports, fitness, business, family, décor, lifestyle, food, entertaining, and so on. Having an assortment on hand can help you expand one another's visions.

It can be surprisingly helpful—and revealing—for partners to determine common goals and values while creating vision boards together. You might even want to try it while you are dating. It's fascinating to see what the other person puts on their board. It can draw you closer together and facilitate encouraging one another toward your goals.

POWER MOVE

View your vision board multiple times a day. The intent behind a vision board is to help you stay focused on your goals and intentions by keeping your most fulfilled life at the forefront of your mind. There is a power and magic in seeing your deepest desires right in front of you every day.

My Vision Board Miracles

Vision boards have made everything I have desired come true in one way or another. And I feel confident that it will continue to work for me as my life continues to evolve. My dream husband, and the experiences and emotions that I wanted from a committed relationship, were up on my board, and now the love that was only exemplified in images has actualized into my real life! Something I yearned for—but wasn't sure I'd ever find—came to me exactly as I dreamt for it to be. What the Universe delivered to me was even better than what I had put up on my vision board.

When I first set a goal of making $100,000 in a year, which was a big climb for my business at the time, I put it up on the board . . . and it happened! Jack Canfield led the way for me with that example. When he said putting $100,000 up on a board worked for him, I thought, *I can do that too!* This just goes back to why it is so important to expand your awareness of possibility and gain exposure to new things in life to ensure that you're expanding your vision.

I've put everything from handbags to cars on my board. And I'm here to tell you, if you want a new home, put that up there too! Amazingly, a house that was on several vision boards I had created for clients completely coincidentally actualized into being my personal home! I didn't even realize it until after we had moved in and owned it for several years. (I tell the full story in my book *Love Coming Home*).

Vision boards certainly should not be limited to themes of financial or material success. It's critical to also represent the feelings and emotions you want to experience. If you want more joy in your life, add images of laughter or other things that tend to induce pleasure and happiness for you. Maybe you value peace and relaxation, and you want to spend more time around water because it calms you. Put up restful images of rivers, lakes, and oceans. You can also include pictures of those specific words, if you like.

Speaking of water, there was a time when I knew I would benefit from drinking more of it. So I put a photo of a refreshing glass of water on my board, along with words and phrases that reminded me of my intention for drinking more water: *bright, shine, great skin, clarity, more energy.* Seeing that daily was so motivating!

The same went for yoga. I put an image of a lovely setting up on the board with someone blissfully experiencing a yoga pose. I added words that exemplified the benefits that I intended to receive through yoga. I also noted the frequency with which I wanted to practice yoga each week. Seeing this made it seem real and doable. And guess what? It was!

I could give so many examples of vision boards working in my life, but I'll share one more that was extra magical. The *Costco Connection* is the most-read magazine in the world, and I had always found its content inspiring. I truly believe that home is the basis for where your best life begins, and I developed a strong desire to contribute a home décor column that would inspire the magazine's readers to get their current homes—their *now* homes—in order so they could love coming home

By chance I cut out a *Costco Connection* article about the CEO of Campbell Soup Company and put it smack-dab in the center of my board. I didn't know what would happen next, but I stared at that photo for a long time before it sparked an awareness: *If I want this, I'd better tell someone I want it! No one will spontaneously knock on my door and offer me space in a magazine if they don't even know I have the desire to be a part of it!* I was scared out of my mind and full of insecurities, but I finally decided to do something about it. Seeing that photo daily was urging me to action.

Finally I emailed someone who knew the publisher of the *Costco Connection,* and I asked if there was any way I could get a meeting with her. Realizing what a huge request I had just made, I was incredibly grateful when my contact person was gracious enough to send the request. Lo and behold, I got the meeting. Fast forward a few months, and I received an email from the editor saying that instead of me submitting a column, they would like me to be their cover story. Blown away doesn't even begin to describe what I was feeling. I get goose bumps just thinking of it. I brought my computer over to one of my employees and asked if they could read the screen, as I thought I must be misreading the email.

When the magazine's reporter, Hana Medina, came to my office to spend the day with me, she noticed my vision board. I felt exposed and embarrassed at first, since she was seeing my cuttings of her magazine right there in front of her. It felt like she was looking at my underwear drawer. Then she pointed out something I hadn't noticed before: I had not just cut out a regular column, I had cut out a cover story about a female CEO! Unknowingly, I had put something on my vision board that was bigger than I ever would have dreamt up on my own . . . and it came true. And my smaller, original goal for a column, which was my huge intention at the time, also ended up coming true, as I now get to contribute home décor columns to the *Costco Connection*.

But be prepared: when you put a dream and intention on your vision board, something even larger than you dared to dream is likely to come true!

Creating a vision board is quite simple. There's no need to overthink it, and no need for perfection. But be prepared: when you put a dream and intention on your vision board, something even larger than you dared to dream is likely to come true!

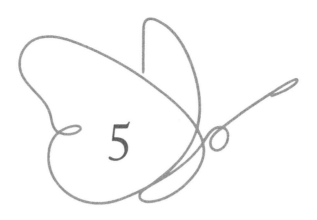

THE POWER OF INTENTIONS AND STEPPING-STONES

The secret of change is to focus all your energy not on fighting the old, but on building the new.

Dan Millman

Awareness of what you truly want, and what most fulfills you, is what will inspire you to passionately seek out and experience your most fulfilled life. That's why the previous chapters on the power to dream big, harness your mind, and create your vision board are so important. Now that you've begun to identify your biggest dreams, it's time to bring organization, intention, focus, and action to them.

Your next step is to identify the deeper meanings and feelings behind each of your goals and dreams so you can harness the power in each of your intentions. We will then explore how to break your intentions into focused, actionable stepping-stones that will guide you along the path to living your dreams today rather than just hoping for them as some far-off wish.

What Is an Intention?

You still might be wondering, *What is an intention?* The word *intention* is widely used and practiced within all walks of life. You might be thinking, *So what does it really mean? And how does it work?* An intention is the motivating factor or the underlying reason behind all that you do, the purpose and desired feelings behind your action. As John Assaraf, one of the contributing teachers in the book, *The Secret*, told me in our conversation, "Intention is the start of focusing and articulating what you want. What would you like to do? Who would you like to be? A goal then turns that intention into something achievable, for instance, by giving it a due date."[21]

As your desire is,
so is your intention.
Upanishads

Like your dreams, your life intentions should be authentic and inspiring to you, originating from your deepest desires. As Deepak Chopra further explains,

> Intention is much more powerful when it comes from a place of contentment than if it arises from a sense of lack or need. Stay centered and refuse to be influenced by other people's doubts or criticisms. Your higher self knows that everything is all right and will be all right, even without knowing the timing or the details of what will happen.[22]

As with your vision board itself, it's up to you whether you share your intentions or choose to keep them private. Sometimes knowing that others will be seeing our intentions and dreams can cause us to subconsciously limit them. We might think, *Who am I to dream this big?* Or, *They will think I'm crazy if they know this is what I want to do!* Thus we limit our options based on potential embarrassment or fear of what others will think of us. Remember to keep in mind that your dreams, intentions, and stepping-stones belong only to you, and that you needn't share them unless you want to.

Before we move on to setting our intentions, I would like to distinguish *goal* from *intention*. Goals are specific, external achievements you hope to accomplish in the future. Intentions are independent of the destination; they are the driving motivator, or the feelings you desire to experience in life in general, or while striving toward your goal. By backing your goal with an intention, you will ensure that the journey is as desirable as the destination. This is key. When you identify your intentions, you ensure the goals you attempt to achieve match up with the feelings and emotions you desire in life.

This metaphor might help clarify the difference between these two words: let's say your goal is to run the New York City Marathon—a huge goal pursued by tens of thousands of runners from all over the world. As you prepare for the race, your intention is to be mindful and present so you experience joy and a sense of accomplishment throughout the whole experience. This helps keep you committed to the hard work that comes with training for a marathon. The intention is all about being present, and enjoying the journey you take from the moment you set that dream for yourself, throughout the months of preparation, and to the moment you cross the finish line and achieve your goal. By being present with your intention, you are living your dream from day one, as the journey is just as inspiring as the actual goal achievement. Thus, you are bringing more fulfillment to your life the very moment you commit to working toward your dream.

Committing Your Dreams, Intentions, and Stepping-Stones to Written Form

For this next part of the process, it is critical to write down your dreams, intentions, and stepping-stones (as you started to do with your big dreams in chapter 2), and merge them all into one single document. Left only in your head, they can become a jumbled, overwhelming mess and make moving toward your dreams feel almost scary. This step in your process is meant to inspire you and help you see how your dreams can take shape. If you want to achieve your dreams, there is no substitution for writing things down.

I can't tell you how many people I talk to who have a dream that has never quite manifested. The first question I ask is whether they have written it down, and 95 percent of the time the answer is no. "But the dream is in my head!" they proudly announce. In your head is not good enough. Yes, we have the power of our minds to initiate or activate our dreams, which is its own act of courage, but the next step to realizing your dream's fulfillment is to commit your intentions and stepping-stones to paper. If that commitment scares you, just breathe and do it anyway! Remember you also hold the power to use your eraser; at any moment you can change what you have written down.

If you have a to-do list for your daily work and personal activities, you know firsthand how much more effective you are at remembering and accomplishing your to-dos when they're out of your head and written all in one spot rather than scattered in separate lists or on sticky notes.

As I wrote earlier on the value of decluttering your mind, creating a list of all the tasks you want to accomplish and keeping it in a centralized place, such as a notebook, reduces anxiety and increases productivity. These results are backed up by recent studies in cognitive science which show that uncluttering your brain by creating specific and comprehensive to-do lists allows for greater creativity and efficiency.[23]

Author David Allen had this insight:

You can train yourself, almost like an athlete, to be faster, more responsive, more proactive, and more focused in dealing with all the things you need to deal with. You can think more effectively and manage the results with more ease and control. You can minimize the loose ends across the whole spectrum of your work life and personal life and get a lot more done with less effort. And you can make front-end decision making about all the stuff you collect and create standard operating procedure for living and working in this millennium. Before you can achieve any of that, though, you'll need to get in the habit of keeping nothing on your mind.[24]

The dreams, intentions, and stepping-stones document we'll be creating together is the most important document you will ever create: We will be creating your to-do list for life! And not just any life. It's the to-do list for your most fulfilling life! You'll be solidifying your goals and dreams with intentions, and building your path to fulfillment through manageable stepping-stones. So it's important to keep track of all of them in one place. This might sound complicated, but it's actually quite simple. And fun to create! So don't overthink it. There is no such thing as perfection here.

As I mentioned in chapter 2, I like to use PowerPoint or Keynote, but when I started the process of writing down my dreams and intentions, I used to use a three-ring binder with a dedicated page for each big dream. That was effective for me at the time.

After years of practice, I now find it much easier to use an electronic document, which not only is easier to edit when I decide to make adjustments but also provides a good basis for re-creation of my lists of dreams and intentions year after year. That's the best part of this process: nothing is set in stone; it's continually evolving.

Electronic documents can make it simpler to review past years and track your progress. I find it somewhat funny (yet encouraging!) to look back on certain dreams that used to cause me so much fear and insecurity, now knowing that they came true years ago and I'm on to bigger, more inspiring dreams that are, sometimes, even scarier!

Step 1: Creating Your Life Intentions Book

Whatever method you choose to keep track of your goals, intentions, and stepping-stones, whether a notebook or an electronic program, this is going to be your only document source for capturing your dreams from this point forward, so use a program or format that you can add pages to. Give it the title *Life Intentions Book*. All of your goals, intentions, and stepping-stones will live in it. This will be your main tool for mapping and achieving your dreams, as it will clearly identify your path to attaining your most fulfilled life.

Step 2: Creating Your Life Intention Statement and Cover Page

Let's begin by setting an overarching life intention. Simply put, it is your mission statement. Similar to what every business creates, only this is for your life. It's your reason for being, your purpose, your deepest desire. Here is an example of what my life intention looks like: *My life intention is to live a life full of love, happiness, abundance, health, and contentment. Inspiring others to greatness is a prominent part of my life because it brings me joy.*

Briefly state, in a sentence or two, your intention for your life. What do you want out of your life, and why? You want it to be something you can memorize and easily recall for your own inspiration, and to answer someone who asks you what you want out of life. Not that you owe anyone else an explanation of what you want, but it should be that easy to remember.

Start your dedicated Life Intentions Book by creating your cover page:

- Title it "My Life Intention."
- Add your name and date.
- Write out your Life Intention Statement.

Remember to keep your life intention brief and in the present tense. Here are some examples to help you begin:

My life intention is to live a life that is full of adventure, freedom, and flexibility. Being physically and mentally fit brings me joy.

My life intention is to live a life doing work that is creative and ever changing. I love having a home filled with joy and spending quality time with my family. It completes me.

My life intention is to live a life that is calm and relaxing. My life is full of stability, and I am clear and living in the moment at all times. This brings me peace.

My life intention is to have a life full of abundance and great health.
Giving back to those in need is a big part of my life because it fills
me with joy.

Again, the life intention you put on your cover page is a brief, concise statement for your life. At first, you may find it challenging to keep your life intention short. That's fine. Right now, if you have a lot to put down, go ahead and write it all. You can always go back to hone it into a more precise statement, which may take time and reflection. At this point the length isn't important. What is important, however, is getting it out of your head and in writing. Your Life Intention Statement will undoubtedly evolve.

It took me a while to get mine to where it felt just right, so don't worry if you continually revise your life intention. That's normal. Now mine hardly ever varies from year to year, as I've been thinking about it for so long. The tactics and goals that I adopt to achieve my intention continue to evolve and grow, but as of late, my intention itself has remained the same.

I recommend adding the date to your cover page. It's inspiring to go back later in life and see your personal evolution. It is something that will never get old.

Step 3: Creating Your Dream Big Table of Contents

Now refer back to your Dream Big List that you created in chapter 2, where you expanded your vision. Using this list, take each of your dreams and wholeheartedly commit to them by putting them on a single page in your Life Intentions Book. This page will go right after your cover page.

This page acts as your table of contents. It's an easy reference to view your main goals and dreams at a glance—in one place.

Step 4: Creating Your Dream Chapters

Next, using your table of contents as your reference, treat each Dream Big List item like a book chapter.

- Create a page for each dream.
- Title the page with the name of that dream.
- Leave plenty of blank space to fill in the driving motivators and intentions behind each dream, and then the stepping-stones needed to actualize each goal. (If you are using a fixed notebook leave blank pages behind each dream in case you need more space to write.)

At this point, you might have ten to fifteen pages. Maybe less, maybe more! You can continue to add or subtract pages at will, but please don't subtract dreams out of fear. We'll circle back to that topic soon and help you move through that all-too-normal feeling that comes along with dreaming big.

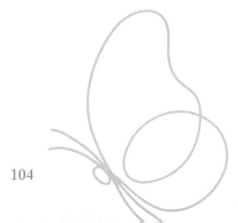

POWER MOVE

Starting with the first dream chapter page you created, read the dream you wrote down, and then tap into your heart for a moment. What are the feelings, and possibly the deeper truths, behind what this dream means to you? Just notice the first thoughts and feelings that come to you.

For example, if your dream is to be a veterinarian, what is the underlying motivator? What benefit would this bring to your life? How would you feel? You might answer:

- Being around animals calms me.
- Helping and caring for animals brings me joy.
- I will have more financial freedom.
- I will be free of a desk job.
- Something new will challenge me every day.

By tapping into your heart center, you can identify the motivating factors and desires behind your dreams, which helps you discover what you truly want now and ways that you can start to live your dreams in the present.

By tapping into your heart center, you can identify the motivating factors and desires behind your dreams, which helps you discover what you truly want now and ways that you can start to live your dreams in the present. It also takes a big dream that feels outlandish or overwhelming and helps you see more clearly how you can actualize it by taking small, practical steps.

Using the example of becoming a veterinarian, if going back to school to get the required education is not something you want, your desires will not feel congruent. By examining the deeper motivations behind your dream—your intention—you will start to see other opportunities to accomplish your dream. Once you realize that the lengthy education process needed to become a veterinarian is not one that would bring you the joy you desire from this goal, it could lead you to explore other options that can provide the same underlying sense of purpose and the lifestyle you deeply want.

Reflect on options that can help you achieve the desired result that lines up with a process that is more appealing to you. Still using the veterinarian dream scenario, consider a variation such as starting a pet day-care facility. Doing this would mean caring for and interacting with animals on a daily basis, all the while freeing yourself from a desk and allowing your financial freedom to be in your own hands based on how little or how much you want to grow your business.

If the process of identifying your intention has caused a slight shift in your big dream, that's what erasers are for! Now's the time to make a slight adjustment to that goal, so that it is more in line with the feelings and emotions you want to experience in life.

Remember that your intention statement should be brief and easy to remember, as it's coming right from your heart. It states your goal combined with the feelings you want to experience. It should be in the present tense, in the form of an action. Make it meaningful to you. And be specific here. This is your dream. Clearly state it.

POWER MOVE

Now we're going to streamline your heart-centering activity into one or two sentences max, and commit it to writing. We will now be creating an intention statement for each of your dreams. This will be written on your dream chapter page, right underneath your dream title.

For example, continuing with our veterinarian example, you realized through further reflection that your dream of becoming a veterinarian has transformed into opening a pet-care business. Creating your intention statement could look something like this: *I'm in the process of creating a pet day-care business that cares for dogs. It challenges, inspires, and provides financial freedom, and flexibility of schedule.*

Using another example, instead of saying that you want to lose twenty pounds, you could instead state your intention as, *I am in the process of becoming the healthiest version of myself. Being healthy gives me the energy to achieve what I want in life, and joy that comes from the confidence I feel when I look and feel my best.*

Positioning your dream intention statement in the form of a present-tense action phrase—"I'm in the process of" as opposed to "I want to"—is important, and we will discuss it more deeply in chapter 6: "The Power of Your Words."

Now solidify your dream intention statement by putting it right onto your dream page. You have just turned your goal into an intention! Doesn't that feel good? Turning your goals into actionable intentions, and then stating them in the present tense as if you already have them, gives your dreams meaning and inspires you to commit. Identifying and continually remembering the way you want to feel (and will feel) from taking action toward your dreams is a powerful motivator.

To set an intention for each dream chapter in your Life Intentions Book, repeat these steps:

- Go through your table of contents and create an individual page for each dream or goal.
- Take each dream and tap into your heart center so you can get clear on what that dream means to you.
- When you have a clearer sense of what it is you desire, turn that dream into an actionable, present-tense intention. Write that intention statement down on your dream page.
- Don't get overly caught up in the wording. If at first this feels overwhelming, simply commit your desired feelings to paper.

Step 5: Building Your Stepping-Stones

Now that you've established your intention to go along with each dream, it's time to identify, in no particular order, every step that you could take to help you get closer to achieving your goal. By creating small, manageable stepping-stones, you can map out a real path that can transform your dream into your reality.

Here are some examples of what your stepping-stones could be:

- Take a specific class or workshop.
- Research what networking resources are available (such as online resources, meet ups, and conferences).
- Practice visualizing the end result you desire as if it were a movie, twice a week.
- Ask someone to be your mentor.
- Shadow someone (for a day) who has accomplished the same goal.
- Save money.
- Create a weekly schedule that carves out time to work toward your goal.

POWER MOVE

Choose one of your dreams. For that specific dream chapter and intention, it's time to list all possible stepping-stones. You don't need to put anything in a specific order at first. Right now the key is to put anything and everything down on paper that you notice from each intention—a major brainstorming list of everything you can think of that would help you get closer to your goal.

What I love about this process is that each stepping-stone is a mini goal soon to be achieved—you are actively in the process of living your dream right now! As you accomplish each stepping-stone you get to cross it off your list. You must be prepared to work hard, but it should also be an inspiring process. Each stepping-stone you accomplish is bringing you closer to your larger goal.

> In truth, one step at a time is not too difficult. . . . I know that small attempts, repeated, will complete any undertaking.
> *Og Mandino*

Another reason I appreciate this process so much is that not only are you getting closer to your dream, but you're in testing mode, which allows you to try your goals on for size. For example, job-shadowing someone who has already fulfilled the dream you are working toward is a great way to ensure that you enjoy the process that goes along with the end result. At any point you can decide to make a goal adjustment, if necessary, before you've gotten too far down a given path.

POWER MOVE

Using the stepping-stone brainstorming list you just created for one of your dreams, it's time to get much more specific! For example, if you need to save cash: how much cash, and how frequently? Going to the gym: where, what time of day, and how often? Job-shadowing someone: who and when?

It's helpful to break things down as specifically as you can. If your big goal is to lose twenty pounds, general stepping-stones might be getting more exercise, eating healthier food, getting more sleep. By adding greater specificity, the list could look something like this:

Lose one pound per week by accomplishing the following.

Eat healthy foods:

- Whole, unprocessed foods
- Non-inflammatory foods
- Low or no sugar

Get more exercise:

- Yoga twice a week. Once at home using an app, and once at the yoga studio.
- Walk three times a week. One day will be three miles around the neighborhood; two days will be two miles on a treadmill during my lunch break.

Drilling down and getting more specific with your intentions is important. How difficult does it sound to lose twenty pounds? Extremely! I know firsthand, as there was a time when I had thirty to lose. When I looked at it in terms of thirty pounds, there was no way it was happening. In fact, it didn't happen for years. But how much more achievable does it sound when you break it down to just one pound at a time?

When you break it down even further, into manageable stepping-stones to get you to that one-pound loss per week, it will make it so much easier and less overwhelming to achieve your goal. You're creating your path by setting mini intentions that coincide with your larger goals in life.

POWER MOVE

Give yourself a deadline or a time frame for when you will accomplish each stepping-stone.

If your goal seems easy, and you're so excited to get it accomplished you can hardly stand it, you don't need to put a timeline to it. I'm confident you will get it done. However, if something feels like more of a grind (weight loss?) and it's something you could easily put off for someday or be too busy to accomplish, you must hold yourself accountable and set timelines. Like the one-pound-per-week guideline. You are accountable for your timeline each week.

Once you set your time frames and the tactics to get you there (such as yoga and walking, as related to your exercise goal), add them to your calendar as you would an appointment. There is something reassuring in knowing you have set aside time to accomplish something. You're putting it into action mode right off the bat! Creating intentions backed up by stepping-stones for all of your goals is key in every aspect of realizing your most fulfilled life.

If you want to attract the perfect partner for you, get specific. What traits do you admire in a partner? Write them down. Sometimes knowing what you *do not* want helps as much as knowing what you do want, so it's okay to create a temporary side list of *do not wants*, as you narrow things down to a powerful *want* list. Coincidentally, both my husband and I had created a list for what we wanted in our perfect partners. On our first date, I was blown away when he said he had a list and pulled it right out of his wallet! My jaw dropped. I hadn't actually brought my list to dinner that night, but I had one too! And he fit it to a T. At that moment I was so grateful that I had created a list to keep me on the right track and that I hadn't compromised on finding a partner who was perfectly suited for me.

Dr. Connie Mariano shares a similar experience: "After twenty-nine years of marriage, I found myself divorced. One of my friends confronted me and said, 'If you really hope to find your soul mate, you have to write down, with extreme specificity, exactly what you want, and you have to put it into your Blackberry and look at it every single day.'"[25]

Finally she did this, and she looked at it every single day. When out of the blue a patient she had had for five years walked into her office and said, "Marry me!" she was rightfully taken aback! He was a nice guy, but she had never given him a thought beyond being her patient. After much pursuit on his part, she finally agreed to a date . . . and it turned out that he was exactly everything she had written down on her list! Connie went on to say, "When you're looking for a true love partner that really suits what you are looking for, it helps to be deliberate about your search."[26]

For your financial goals, break it down to the exact dollar amount you want to make, as well as the exact dollar amount you want to save—short term and long term. And give yourself a time frame for when you will achieve those goals. This is a powerful tool for getting ahead financially.

One of my mentors, Eli Morgan, was raised by a single mom with limited resources, yet he was able to achieve major success in the insurance business. He cofounded M Financial Group in Portland, Oregon, which grew to have more than 155 member firms: in forty US states, Switzerland, the United Kingdom, and the United Arab Emirates. M Financial is one of the nation's leading financial services design and distribution companies.

Eli repeatedly reminded me to get extremely specific with my financial goals, and to dream big, even when my design company was still quite small. He inspired me by reminding me that as he was growing his company from $0, he set a major-stretch goal for himself of making $5,000 a month. Before long, he did it! So then he added another $5,000, making it $10,000, and after that he upped it yet another $5,000. He continued that process until he was taking home $40,000 a month and his company grew exponentially from there. He also stated this goal in the present tense and backed it with intention. In its first iteration, he gave the financial goal a why: "I thoroughly enjoy having $5,000 to deposit into my checking account each month." He truly feels that setting stretch goals, writing them down, giving them a why (intention), and stating them in the present tense (as if he already had that $5,000) kept them at the top of his mind and made them ultimately achievable.

Practice Makes Perfect

When you're first starting off, you will want to read your dreams, intentions, and stepping-stones continually: every day for the first month. It will only take a few minutes. You need them to stay at the top of your mind, as they will influence your choices and decisions on a daily basis. As with a to-do list, if you don't look at it, the items on the list don't seem to get done.

As choices and potential commitments come up, even if they seem like worthy causes, ask yourself, *Will this commitment get me closer to my goal?* If not, having your list should make it much easier to take a pass. You have a lot to accomplish. Your stepping-stones list can help guide the choices you make in regard to how to use your time and better ensure that you don't get sidetracked by distractions.

After the first few months, you can start to look at your stepping-stones twice a week, but please stay disciplined, and don't do it any less frequently than that. Sundays tend to be a good day for me to review mine. It inspires me for the week ahead. I'm also in a more relaxed, receptive space. Pick the day of the week on which you tend to feel the most open and inspired. Then pick your second day, one on which you typically need a pick-me-up and could easily slack off due to being tired from the week—maybe a Wednesday afternoon.

Using your Life Intentions Book in conjunction with your Dream Big Vision Board is empowering. You are seeing your goals in written form and in the form of real images that exemplify it having come true. If through the process of writing down your dreams, intentions, and stepping-stones you made subtle shifts to your dreams, make sure to reflect those shifts in the images you have on your board. Your Dream Big Vision Board and Life Intentions Book should mirror and complement each other, working together in unison as a transformational tool that embodies the fulfilling life you desire. And remember to also practice visualization and play your dreams out in your mind as if they were a true-life movie. These three tools—the Dream Big Vision Board, the Life Intentions Book, and visualization—when used together, make a uniquely powerful combination.

Doing this keeps you focused on your goal. It is so easy to get distracted by another shiny object and be thrown off course. Using these power moves lessens that temptation, even subconsciously. The good thing is that if you do get off course, you can get back on, right where you left off.

Building your path through setting intentions backed by stepping-stones is a critical and inspiring part of the process.

Building your path through setting intentions backed by stepping-stones is a critical and inspiring part of the process. Committing your dreams and intentions to paper and building your path through identifying your stepping-stones are crucial to the process. I can't emphasize this enough. Do not allow your dreams, intentions, and stepping-stones to live only in your head. There is power in putting pen to paper, or fingers to a keyboard.

You have just identified actions you can start doing today! So start them! Today! Your future self will thank you! I think of this every time I need a little kick in the pants: your future best self begins by being your best right now. Maybe that will help you too. Just begin! By beginning you are in active pursuit of your dreams. You are living them as we speak, and you are now well on your way to accomplishing your goals.

POWER MOVE

Now that you're writing down your dreams, intentions, and stepping-stones, commit to reading them every day so they stay at the forefront of your mind. As you encounter choices on a daily basis, ask yourself—every single time—will this get me closer to my dream?

Now begin! Pick one stepping-stone today and accomplish it! Then pick another, and another, and another . . .

THE POWER OF
YOUR WORDS

Whatever is expressed is impressed.
Whatever you say to yourself, with
emotion, generates thoughts, ideas and
behaviors consistent with those words.

Brian Tracy

How you use your words, what you choose to say, and the conversations you have matter when striving to manifest your dreams and deepest desires. This applies to verbal communication in person or by phone, as well as email, text, and social media. Even the words you say or think to yourself matter!

In times past verbal words mattered most, but let's face it, I bet 70 percent of what we say now is in written form. For many, it's more convenient to type than to talk face-to-face.

Your words have power beyond what you might believe. I remember making one of my biggest requests of all time. Meredith Corporation is a powerhouse media and marketing company that owns TV stations around the country and major magazines such as *Better Homes & Gardens* and *Martha Stewart Living.* They also owned the TV show I was currently on, *The Better Show.* I decided to ask one of their executives if Meredith Corporation would partner with me on the marketing of my bedding line. A huge request! But with nothing to lose, I was at least able to secure the meeting.

I flew from the West Coast to New York, in the days when New York was an extravagant and rare trip for me. During the flight I was on pins and needles. I had a lot riding on this proposal, and I knew it was lofty and perhaps highly unlikely. Furthermore, I wasn't wholly confident that the meeting would actually happen, as meetings can tend to get postponed or rescheduled right before they're about to happen. Executives at this level tend to have a packed schedule, and this person had no idea that I had come all this way just for my meeting with him. And being low on the totem pole to him, I worried that should the meeting be postponed, it would be a stretch to think he'd be able to find additional time that day. All of this made me extremely nervous.

Thankfully, my meeting stayed as scheduled, though I will never forget the conversation. As I was finishing up my partnership proposal, the executive asked a pivotal question: Was I planning to launch my bedding line even if I did not secure Meredith Corporation's support? It hit me then that he had sensed my insecurity based on the words I was using! Even though I had what I thought to be a rock-solid presentation, I had been using *someday* and *maybe* words. Not confidence-building whatsoever!

I changed my tune and answered with a resounding YES. And then I told him my launch date! He in turn said yes to our partnership. Before he was willing to move forward, he needed to know that I was confident in my ability to pull this off independent of his company's role.

I learned from that conversation, and it has forever changed the way I communicate. No more will I waffle back and forth with my words. If I intend to do something, my words have to match my intention. The lack of confidence that showed up in my words almost cost me an incredible opportunity to market my bedding line to the world. That day was a major victory, one that I am incredibly grateful for. Had I answered, "Probably," or "I think so," I know I would have gotten a no that day, and he wouldn't have given my proposal another thought.

If others see you as confidently owning your goals and deepest desires they will be more likely to support your efforts. And equally as important is what that confidence does for you! It puts you in the powerful mind-set of *now*. "I should" or "I wish" are someday phrases, not *now* phrases. A big part of the purpose behind having goals and intentions is to feel inspired in life. You don't want to wait until you've accomplished the entire goal to experience inspiration; you'd be missing out on the greatest joy of all, the journey. Live it, be it, *now*.

When you are inspired by some great
purpose, some extraordinary project,
all your thoughts break their bonds,
your mind transcends limitations,
your consciousness expands in every
direction, and you find yourself in a
new, great, and wonderful world.

Wayne Dyer

Using Action Words

Now that you have identified your dreams and goals, set intentions, established a path through stepping-stones, and begun to create a vision board, you are in the process of realizing your most fulfilled life. Congratulations! The next step is to empower all of that with your words!

Your words can put you in a position of power.

Your words can put you in a position of power. For instance, instead of saying, *I should . . . I wish I could*, substitute, *I'm in the process of . . . I'm actively pursuing . . .* anytime you talk about your intentions, whether to yourself or to others. Not that you need to impress others, but having the support of those around you undoubtedly helps.

Always be in *action mode* and in the *now* when talking about your intentions. For example, if your goal is to lose weight, instead of saying, *I am so fat! I shouldn't be eating this!* Practice saying instead, *I'm in the process of getting to my goal weight; I'll pass on eating that right now.* If you desire a new job, instead of saying, *I hate my job! I wish I could be doing something different,* say, *I am working on getting my dream job as a . . .* Own your process!

POWER MOVE

When you use words in action mode and in the now every time you talk about your dreams and intentions, this causes a big shift in the kind of energy you put out, and in how you view yourself. It is uplifting to know you are actively in pursuit of your most fulfilled life. And you are! So own it.

As John Assaraf wisely shared with me, "When you state your intentions using the present tense, you create and reinforce an affirmation, and with repetition, you can create a new neural pattern in your brain. That positive pattern will then become imprinted and automatic. It will also help you to override the voice of your inner critic."[27]

Talk Positively

Always, always, always speak about yourself in a positive light! Always! Many of us, including me, have dealt with that inner voice that likes to shame and criticize. If we listen to that inner bully, our words, thoughts, and bodies start to embody those self-sabotaging feelings. By putting ourselves down with shaming phrases like, *I am so dumb . . . I am an idiot . . . I am not worthy or deserving . . . I will never achieve my dream*, we can ultimately harm ourselves. Self-talk like that makes it hard to get past your limiting beliefs and open yourself up to new opportunities and possibilities. If you're continually putting yourself down, manifesting your positive intentions can seem downright impossible.

Taking full ownership of negative self-talk will make a huge difference in how you see the world, and will ultimately determine your success.

We all know people who regularly use negative self-talk. We might even recognize it in ourselves. Those who continually shame themselves may use phrases such as, *I always get the short end of the stick* or, *I never get the lucky breaks like everyone else* or, *Why do bad things always happen to me?* Does any of this sound familiar? Remember the powerful law of attraction! Saying negative things about yourself, inside or out loud to the world, will only draw more negative circumstances to you.

Taking full ownership of negative self-talk will make a huge difference in how you see the world, and will ultimately determine your success. Even if such negativity has been your pattern in the past, it need not define you going forward. By making a conscious shift, by being present with your words and letting go of all the negative things you say and think about yourself, you can redirect not only your words but also your life. You can open yourself up to experiencing all-new possibilities.

Try being mindful and present with your words for a while; you might be surprised to hear what comes out of your mouth when referring to yourself—negativity you had no idea you were speaking. The good news is that you have the ability to shift this pattern, and it starts inside you. It starts with accepting yourself, and not letting your past or your current circumstances control your *now*. Accepting your past and letting go of limiting beliefs and patterns opens you up to the possibility of creating your most fulfilled life.

It wasn't until I saw the beauty of my upbringing that I was able to release my limiting beliefs and negative self-talk. For years I carried around deep-seated insecurities. Never feeling smart enough, thin enough, or engaging enough—you name it. If it was negative, I felt it. I felt painfully inferior to everyone I encountered. I was stuck in the mind-set of a girl coming from a very small town, who didn't have the same nice clothes, money, car, or home as others. I was uneducated beyond high school in the traditional sense, and I viewed all of these things as limitations. I put a ceiling on what I could accomplish in my life.

What I didn't realize at the time was that my upbringing was the launching pad for my best life to begin! Growing up in humble surroundings taught me to be resourceful. It taught me to work hard for everything that I had. My parents showed me an incredible example of creating a home environment where we could thrive despite not having any money. My upbringing was the basis for my entire business! And it was the backdrop to writing my dream-come-true book *Love Coming Home*, as I know firsthand that you can set up your home environment to support you with very limited resources.

I used to never publicly talk about my upbringing, but once I quit shaming myself for it and shifted to gratitude, my negative self-talk, and the way I talked about my self to others, shifted, and in turn, my life changed. No one was making me feel small; I was doing that to myself! And it was in turn sending off strong vibes of insecurity.

Now I realize what a beautiful part of the countryside we lived in, what an amazing backdrop our small home gave us, and how my resourceful parents taught me to work hard. And when I think about it, the isolation and lack of exposure to the rest of the world for so many years taught me to be very comfortable being on my own, which has also turned into a source of comfort and confidence, as opposed to being a bad thing. When I get sad about missing my sister, my very best friend in the entire world, I turn to gratitude and think about the joy I got to experience from the bond we had. I remember her constant lighthearted nature, and it reminds me to lighten up when I get too serious about life. My past is now my opportunity. It's my opportunity for my very best life! Shifting my negative self-talk also shifted the energy I was giving off into the world.

Dr. Gail Brenner is a world-renowned psychologist who has studied the effects of shaming and the transformative power of truly accepting and loving ourselves for who we are right now:

Rediscovering the full magnificence of who you are is radical, fierce, and loving. All of your hidden feelings are offered the space to be in the deepest acceptance. You don't have to be concerned about changing anything about yourself. Simply welcome what is, as it is, fully. That's all. When you feel fear, it no longer drives you. When you meet shame and lack with clear seeing, you live from wholeness that has never been broken or damaged. . . . Insights appear; new choices come to mind. You constantly emerge fresh and new, unhampered by the past. You're here! Awake, alive, unendingly resilient.[28]

Remember, we are all human. We all encounter hardships and make mistakes sometimes. This book is all about taking ownership of our actions, so take responsibility and move on without shaming yourself. It doesn't do you, or anyone else for that matter, any good when you refer to yourself in a negative manner. Allow the wonderfulness of you to shine with every word that comes out of your mouth. It will draw more wonderfulness to you. It all starts with you.

POWER MOVE

Frame your words in a positive light. Always! You can make a simple shift by reflecting your self-love in the words you say about yourself.

You've probably heard someone (maybe yourself) say, *I am broke, so I can't . . .* , like it's an anchor that has sunk to the bottom of the ocean and will permanently hold them down. Is that seriously the state you want for yourself? Does anyone want that? That state of lack will become the energy you exude in the world and in your body, which is not conducive to creating a healthy, fulfilling life! How much more empowering does it sound if you rephrase that as, *I am in the process of reorganizing my finances, so right now I'm choosing to not spend money on . . .* That identifies it, in your mind and in the minds of others, as a passing phase that you are taking responsibility for. It's not you; it's only your current circumstance, which you are working through on your way to more prosperous times.

Positive words about yourself create a positive mind-set and put you in the driver's seat for success in whatever you want to accomplish in your life.

Positive words about yourself create a positive mind-set and put you in the driver's seat for success in whatever you want to accomplish in your life. Plus you become a more positive person. It takes a little bit of practice, but before you know it, this will become routine. This nuanced speech helps you get beyond your limiting beliefs and behaviors and can be implemented this very second. I've said it before and I'll say it again: remember the law of attraction. Speak about yourself in phrases that you want reflected back to you.

Positive self-talk has lasting effects. Psychologist Ann Kearney-Cooke says, "The way you talk to yourself affects how you feel and how you behave. . . . Positive self-talk can be beneficial. When you are doing it over and over and over again it can rewire the brain."[29]

Your voice activates a release when you state your dream out loud—a liberating feeling of getting something off your chest.

Say Your Dreams Out Loud

One empowering action I love to take is to say my dreams out loud. If you have privacy right now, give it a try. State one of your intentions, in action mode and in the present tense . . . out loud! Go for it! Wasn't that exhilarating? Or maybe a little scary at first? But wow, I bet you felt a surge of energy in your body. Your voice activates a release when you state your dream out loud—a liberating feeling of getting something off your chest. Now say it again, and own it! Dr. Connie Mariano says, "I dream out loud!"[30] when referring to one of the tools she uses to make her biggest dreams come true.

Glenn Stearns told me this story of speaking his intentions out loud:

I remember it being so hard to get started. I was a loan officer and I had my territory. I would walk into real estate offices and ask for business. There were thousands of nos. I was always being ignored. It was hard on my confidence.

When I was at my lowest, I would drive down Pacific Coast Highway and yell out the window, 'I will own you one day!' to the house on the hill. Fifteen years later I passed on buying that home for an even better one.[31]

Stating my dreams out loud is something I learned from my husband, whom I met later in life, once we both had established our businesses. It's rewarding to have a loving partner and collaborator, and I get to learn a lot by listening to stories of his triumphs and failures in addition to my own! He started an international steel-trading company from the ground up with little savings or support around him, and was able to take it to extraordinary heights. When he wanted something, he would state his goal or dream out loud to solidify it and hold himself accountable. Saying it out loud allowed him to shine a light on any negativity or doubt he was harboring, and it would always get him to a more positive, confident state.

At first when I practiced saying my dreams out loud, it felt awkward. I would feel shy and embarrassed, but that soon turned into exhilaration, followed by empowerment. Now sometimes when I have an epiphany or a new idea, I can't wait to get some privacy so I can say it out loud. Just like when I practice for a speaking engagement, saying things out loud—rather than keeping it all in my head— helps me shake out the insecurities. The same is true with my goals. The more I say them out load, the more confident I become in my ability to pull them off.

There's something about stating your goals and dreams out loud that makes them feel more real. It lends a certain type of energy. Say them everywhere. When you're driving, in the shower, looking into the mirror. Shout your intentions from the hilltops when you're hiking, or on a busy road as you're biking. Let it out!

POWER MOVE

State your dreams and your intentions out loud. Do this at least twice a day!

It can also be incredibly powerful to say your intentions out loud to the Universe, God, Spirit, or any source consistent with your spiritual beliefs. You can say them in a prayer. When. Dr. Connie Mariano has a big dream, she surrenders her dream to a higher power: "I visualize my goal and then surrender it to God. If it is meant to be, I will achieve the goal plus more. That is God's signature, when you not only reach your goal but beyond and better than what you imagined."[32]

If you're comfortable doing so, you can say your intentions out loud in front of others, but pick your spots. Make sure you're around a supportive person who wants what's best for you and won't try to belittle or diminish your dream. Hopefully you are fortunate enough to be surrounded by a supportive family and group of friends, but that isn't always the case for everyone.

A Word on Privacy

The owner of the design trade school I attended years ago, Jan Springer, used to remind our class that sometimes the ones who are the closest to us only know us for where we are today, and they can't see our visions as clearly as we can. They aren't going through all the hard work that we're putting in to making our dreams a reality, so without even realizing it, they can sometimes be less of a support than what you need at the time. Her advice is something I still keep in mind.

Without even meaning to hold you back, sometimes your big goals can make others feel guilty for not going for it themselves; unknowingly, they may not be the best ones to support your big dreams. That doesn't mean you are on the wrong path. If they know you today as a receptionist, they might not have the confidence in your skill set just yet to consider you a viable option to design their homes (which is what happened to me). Sometimes you have to go outside your immediate circle of influence when talking about your new endeavor.

It's also fine to keep your dreams private at first. There is no need to share them out loud with anyone besides yourself. Only do it if you feel supported, and when you do, frame your intentions positively and use action-oriented, present-tense words. Like your vision boards, it's up to you to decide if or when you want to share them. Whatever you choose to do, own your words, your dreams, and your intentions when you say them out loud to yourself or anyone else. Let your light shine bright, whether in privacy or in front of a supportive friend or mentor.

Asking for What You Want

This could quite simply be the one thing that has moved me forward in life more than anything else, and one thing everyone I interviewed for this book had in common: they were not afraid to ask the questions that needed to be asked in order to propel their dreams forward. They did not hide on the sidelines hoping for their dreams and goals to miraculously be granted to them. We all need to take complete ownership of ourselves, but in reality, none of us gets to where we want to go entirely on our own. We all need a little assistance—sometimes, a lot of assistance!—to make things happen.

At times, asking for help or advice of any kind can be paralyzing. I continually remind myself, *If you don't ask, you don't give someone the opportunity to give you a yes!* How powerful is that!

If you don't ask, you are guaranteed the answer is no, and you are no better off than where you were. Give people the opportunity to help you by asking questions.

Susan Feldman, cofounder of One Kings Lane, offered this on the topic of asking for what you want, "As awkward as it feels, if it will help you get from point A to point B, you have to rise above the awkwardness of it all, and push yourself to ask the question."[33]

If you don't ask, you are guaranteed the answer is no, and you are no better off than where you were. Give people the opportunity to help you by asking questions. Make requests. State what you want and need! No one can read your mind. It's so easy to let negative self-talk about asking for what you need stop you in your tracks and render you speechless, when a simple question could have gotten you a yes!

When I asked Ginnie Roeglin, then Costco senior vice president of e-commerce, publishing, travel, and marketing, about her perspective on asking for what you want, she gave this helpful insight into what helped her career trajectory:

> Sometimes you need to be the one to propose a new position for yourself. Identify a need you can fill, the value you bring, and ask for what you want. That's how I got some of the biggest upward momentum in my career. I was not given a yes every time I asked, and you might not [be] either, but it shows your superiors that you have ambition and the drive to advance, which can open up future possibilities. Ask the questions, even if at first it feels uncomfortable. You still have to make yourself do it![34]

Sometimes it's even tough to ask the simple questions that help you take better care of yourself. I learned a painful lesson by not asking a simple question about rescheduling something that would have helped me out, simply because I was too afraid to disappoint someone. It was a painful and costly lesson. I was the on-air interior designer for eight seasons on the syndicated lifestyle TV program, *The Better Show*. Early on they would only trust me to be on-air with a host, not on my own. Then, out of the blue, the executive producer decided that she could finally send me out into the field alone. No host; just me! The pressure! But I was up for the challenge, and I was so excited.

A week before I was to film, I had a terrible skiing accident. I tore my ACL and both menisci, and broke my fibula bone. I was in a tremendous amount of pain. My surgery had been scheduled for two weeks later in order to let my broken bone heal first. I was too afraid to tell my producer for fear the rescheduling would inconvenience her and she would not give me another opportunity like that again. And to make matters worse, my filming was scheduled in Palm Desert, California, which required flying.

Too afraid to ask a simple question, whether I could reschedule, I stuck to the filming date. This meant I had to fly with crutches and a massive leg brace. Once I arrived, I had to rent a car, attempt to drive, and shop in a mall, alone and on crutches, to find super-wide pants to cover my leg brace. I cringe just remembering that day.

When it came time to stand up and actually talk to the camera the next day, I had to drop my crutches and balance on one leg. I was frozen in one spot, as I couldn't move around to show anything. And mind you, demonstrating décor tips on location requires walking around and showing off the home to exemplify the talking points. It was terrible.

When the editor got the tapes, he showed them to the producer, who wasted no time in calling me. She wanted to know what was wrong with me that day, that I hadn't been talking or acting at all like myself! And she was right. It was terrible footage, and basically unusable. I had put myself though substantial pain and cost the show a significant amount of money to produce a segment that couldn't be used. And it could all have been preempted if I'd had the courage to ask a simple question. Fortunately, the producer forgave me and I got another shot, but being afraid to ask a question could have ended my career on TV.

Always ask, or communicate what you need. We so often put ourselves in harm's way because we are afraid to inconvenience or disappoint someone else.

Glenn Stearns, founder of Stearns Lending, has a powerful example of asking for help:

> When I started my company I realized it was harder than I ever thought. I was going to fail. I walked into a government office and asked the receptionist how I could get their business. She said I needed a contract, but I didn't know what a contract was. I asked her if she would help me since I didn't know anyone else. That receptionist called me months later and told me a contract was coming up and helped me learn how to submit my proposal. I submitted, won, and I ended up being the largest contractor in the country. It was all from asking the receptionist. In my eyes, she ended up being the most powerful woman in government![35]

When you don't completely understand something, it is easy to allow negative self-talk to creep in. You may see yourself as unqualified and feel embarrassed by your lack of knowledge, so you simply walk away from a potential opportunity. Please know there is no shame in not having all the answers yourself. You'd be amazed how often people are willing to rally around and help the underdog. Admit when you don't understand, and ask for further clarification. You must muster up the courage and ask so you can learn and grow. Everyone has to start somewhere.

Another defining moment for me that illustrates the importance of asking is when my company's bedding line got on the retail map by landing on One Kings Lane, an online home décor company. It was shortly after their revolutionary site had launched. I remember being afraid to make the call to ask if we could sell our product with them. I believed we would get a no, as I was used to nos at that point, and with my confidence at a low point, I hardly felt deserving of selling my bedding on their site. Yet, I knew if I didn't ask, they would have no way of knowing that my bedding line even existed.

Once again, being as optimistic as I could, and knowing I had to take the chance, I finally reached out. When I did, it turns out that they were looking for a high-quality bedding vendor at that very moment, and I had just enough inventory to meet their requirements in the time frame they needed. In fact, mine ended up being the first foundational bedding collection sold on One Kings Lane. In the first seventy-two hours, we sold $56,000 worth of bedding! Had I not asked, we would not have realized that revenue. Then, after each subsequent flash sale, the sales continued to get better and better. Had I not gotten beyond my limiting beliefs and asked, we would not have gotten that first yes, which ultimately led to more (and larger) doors opening up for my company.

Ask for what you want! Give someone the ability to answer you with a yes. Don't keep your desires hidden away for someday.

Getting the mentors you want and need in life is closely tied to the power of your words. It is all about the way you communicate your request.

The Art of Gaining a Mentor

Do you need mentors? Yes! You need a lot of them and for all different purposes. Do they need to know they're your mentors? Not necessarily. The person you will undoubtedly benefit from the most is probably so busy they don't have time for mentorship, and the mere question can send them running for the hills, away from one more obligation! Getting the mentors you want and need in life is closely tied to the power of your words. It is all about the way you communicate your request.

Having mentors has been extraordinarily helpful in my life. There is no way I would be where I—in any aspect of my life—am were it not for the help of mentors, and plenty of them. Pretty much everything I have learned has been passed down from a mentor of some sort. And I've never had just one dedicated mentor, as the people I respect and go to for advice typically aren't experts in all areas of life. Hardly anyone is, for that matter. Even most attorneys and doctors have specific areas of expertise.

I use a variety of mentors for different topics and different situations, and at the time I need them. For example, when wanting to lose weight, I went to someone who had effectively shed weight in a healthy manner. When I wanted to expand my business nationally and have design offices in two states, I sought out someone who understood my industry and the size of my business, and had been in a similar situation. When I was first starting out and didn't know how to read a spreadsheet, I found someone who possessed that skill, and when it came time that I needed to learn how to read a profit and loss statement, I found someone who had strong experience in reading them. The mentor I would call upon to give me feedback on how to maintain a loving marriage is not necessarily the same person I would go to for financial advice.

Susan Feldman has a great take on how to find mentors in life:

> Networking is key. Meet as many people as you can, and then try to create ongoing relationships with several individuals who can help you in different areas. This way you won't have to rely on just one person, and you will be able to leverage different individuals' expertise. Don't actually say to someone, *Will you be my mentor*; instead, build a network of many, and build relationships.[36]

This not only ensures that you're getting the right kind of advice for the topic you are seeking but also reduces the obligation of any one mentor.

The secret to convincing mentors to help you is actually to not ask them to be your mentor. Why? Because when you ask someone to be your mentor, you are likely to get a quick no due to his or her lack of time. People we tend to want as mentors undoubtedly have packed schedules and goals of their own, and they have learned the art of saying no to anything that could distract them from their purpose.

First and foremost, do your homework. Identify someone who has shown a great example of doing exactly what it is you want to accomplish with your life, whether it be a loving relationship, an amazing job of parenting, or a great track record in a similar business—choose your advisor carefully. You should not go to your coworker for advice simply because he or she is a convenient listening ear. Go to the source of knowledge on whatever topic you desire to learn more about.

Choose someone you deeply respect. Let it be someone you feel is a big stretch to even ask for advice. The main reason being that if you take your time and their time, it had better be worth it. The worst thing you can do is ask someone for advice knowing you don't fully trust or respect the advice they are about to give you. If you go to the wrong source, not only is it going to waste time for both of you, but it could send you down the entirely wrong path.

As I said before, you can identify a multitude of mentors for different life situations. It doesn't need to be only one person. I've had countless mentors along my journey—some at the same time—and I will surely continue to need them as I discover new and more fascinating ways to grow. Find mentors who have shown a track record of success in whatever it is you are trying to do.

When you have identified that person, make it easy for them to give you a yes. Invite them to coffee or lunch, but don't keep it general or too social, like you're trying to be their friend. Give it a purpose, with a finite start and stop time. State your reason up front, and why you are asking them and not someone else. This will make it personal. Most people want to help others, but no one wants to waste their time.

POWER MOVE

My Favorite Tips on Gaining a Mentor

When you call or email your potential mentor, here are a few suggestions for getting a yes:

- *Keep it brief.*

- *Address the person with respect. You can mention what you specifically respect about the person.*

- *State your goal clearly. For example, I am in the process of . . .*

- *Invite the person to coffee or lunch: I'd like to take you to coffee or lunch for forty-five minutes, and I promise to respect that time frame.*

- *Name the topic you want to ask for advice on.*

- *Did I mention to keep it brief? If your communication is in writing, delete as many extra words or sentences as you can.*

- *If you're emailing, double-check that the email address and spelling of the person's name are correct. Make sure your subject line reflects the topic. And unless you are already on friendly terms, don't use emojis.*

The person you are seeking advice from is probably so busy they can hardly sneak in a moment of personal time as it is, and more than likely they don't need more friends, so a lunch invitation alone is not going to tempt them. If you state your purpose up front, relate it back to their expertise, and qualify why you are worthy of their time—because you are going somewhere in life—they will more than likely have a soft spot in their heart for you. It won't feel like a long-term commitment, and they may recall a time when someone else helped them out. A request for forty-five minutes with defined parameters is much easier to ask for than a full-blown mentorship. Remember to say, *I am in the process of* . . . rather than *I want to* . . . That shift in your words is much more intriguing to a potential mentor. It shows that you are taking responsibility for your goals, and that their time will be put to good use.

When you get a yes to your lunch date, which I'm confident you will, get right to the point. Remember that this person isn't there with you to gain another friend, nor to open up about their weekend plans. Please don't waste their time by broadly asking them how they got to where they are today. Do your research beforehand, and instead pay them a specific compliment or ask them targeted questions that show you are knowledgeable and respectful of their path in life.

Stick to the time frame you requested. And take notes! It shows you care. If you know for sure you have chosen a mentor who has had success in the undertaking you desire, pay attention to what this person says. You shouldn't follow blindly, but do take in their feedback. Not only is it respectful, but you can also gain valuable knowledge from someone who has charted a similar course before you.

After you leave, always follow up with a thank-you note and a brief update on your progress. Mentors love knowing when they have made a positive impact on your life. And it will open them up to helping you in the future. Even if, after talking with them, you decide to go down a different path, it's still important to follow up. If you opt to change course, you can say something like, *I took to heart what you said, and I decided to change course. Thank you for helping me discover a different path and not waste any more time. I'm now in the process of . . .*

The right mentors have moved mountains for me in my life. I feel so grateful to have encountered so many generous souls and brilliant minds along my journey. I would not be where I am right now, in any aspect of my life or my business, had I not been around so many positive, uplifting, candid, emotionally and intellectually talented people. But it all started by asking! None of the mentors I've been fortunate enough to spend time with would have necessarily sought me out. I can tell you firsthand, it is a scary feeling to ask someone of a significant caliber, in any aspect of life, for some of their time. But the trade-off is so worth it. And the beautiful thing is that most people who have reached a certain level of success in their lives are more than happy to help you soar too.

As Susan Feldman went on to share:

When I first came up with the idea for One Kings Lane I was introduced to Lisa Stone, the cofounder of the site, BlogHer.com. In fact, that's how I met my partner, Ali. The first thing Lisa asked me was, "How can I help you?" She was so busy, and was so accomplished, yet she wanted to help me. Lisa's words and willingness to help made such an impression on me. Today I try to always pay it forward and give my time to others when they ask. If we help each other, we will all get much further in life. [37]

Getting a Yes through Email

Do you experience times when the questions or requests you make in an email go unanswered? Your points don't seem to get across, and it feels almost as if the recipient didn't read your email in its entirety? That can be frustrating, especially when you're working so hard to make all of your life dreams come true, and you were hoping for an answer on something.

Well, chances are that if you've sent a lengthy email, it's probably what it seems to be: the recipient didn't read it entirely. Or maybe they started to read it but got distracted and then forgot to go back to it. Our attention span for reading emails shortened the moment Twitter came up with the brilliant idea that we could get our points across in 280 characters or less (which was increased from its original 140-character limit). If you really try, typically you can! Learning the art of making a request via email is helpful when trying to move any dream forward.

Unless you're sending an old-fashioned love letter to a long-lost soulmate, no matter how passionate you are about your topic, you have a much better chance of the recipient actually reading it and responding if you keep your message brief and follow a few tried-and-true email protocols.

POWER MOVE

My Favorite Email Tips

- *Keep your emails brief.*

- *Stick to one topic per email.*

- *Have the subject line reflect the topic.*

- *Get right to the point.*

- *Don't bury the lead! State your request right up front, or if it has to be at the end, highlight it with bold text.*

- *Use short paragraphs. Break up the copy so your eye dances across the page.*

- *Use bullet points if you have multiple takeaways; make them easy to read at a glance.*

- *Save the pleasantries till the end, if you even need them at all.*

- *Triple-check any names in the cc field.*

- *Ask yourself whether each person on the list unquestionably needs this information; if not, delete.*

- If the topic changes throughout the email trail, revise the subject line, or start a new email thread.

- Lastly, pay attention to the written words you use. Until this becomes routine, anytime you are texting or emailing about yourself, try reading it out loud. Are you being positive? Or are you slipping into negative self-talk?

If you find yourself ending an email with *Sorry for the long email*, go back and rework it. Can you break the email into a few separate emails so the recipient can fire back quick responses to each topic?

Have you ever hit send too early and caused yourself embarrassment? If you're typing a sensitive email of any kind, delete all recipients from the "To" field. Take the time to draft the email until you're satisfied with what you've written, and then purposely insert each recipient one by one. This sounds like a pain, but it is worth it to save yourself the embarrassment of sending off an email that doesn't convey your whole intent or is unwittingly sent to the wrong person. Being impatient can cause you to overlook the details and make mistakes that don't present you or your request in the best light.

These few Power Moves will help you ensure that the intention behind your written words comes across clearly and succinctly and, most important, that you get a response to whatever it is you are asking.

Courageous Conversations

Did you think you were getting out of this one? Nope! Though we dread them, courageous conversations move mountains. If you're willing and able to have them—with everyone—you will see major change in your life.

Let's be clear: courageous does not mean confrontational. I know plenty of people who thrive on confrontation. I'm not one of them. I used to struggle with fitting in, so much so that the last thing I wanted to do was have a courageous conversation, let alone a confrontational one. I would do anything to accommodate the other person, to avoid inconveniencing them or ruffling any feathers. That didn't do me or anyone else any good.

Courageous conversation means having conversations that need to be had. Instead of letting yourself stew about something for hours, days, or months, take responsibility and action. The sooner you can have the conversations you need to have, whether it be in business or in your personal life, the sooner you will be free to let the good flow into your life. We burn considerable mental energy thinking about the conversations we don't have, but should, and it is a waste of our valuable headspace. By using your words to have courageous conversations, you free up your valuable energy to think about the exciting new goals and intentions you're fulfilling. It gives you the mental space to strategize and process the good.

Courageous conversations bring about good things. It doesn't mean having an argument or proving that you're right and the other person is wrong. A candid, straightforward conversation allows you to clear your mind, get to the heart of the matter, and bring conclusion to a lingering situation or a matter that needs discussing in order to reach the result you desire. Simply put, they allow you to move forward in life.

Deborah Rowland, who has been an executive with major corporations such as PepsiCo, Shell, and BBC Worldwide, whote an article for the *Harvard Business Review* with this perspective on courageous conversations:

> I've learned that in leadership roles the most important work often happens in the least comfortable spaces. Handled well, risky and confrontational conversations—especially those that surface awkward facts or get to the source of organizational tensions—can improve how we relate to each other . . . and enable leaders to make better decisions. . . . Safety is perilous, and difficulty is strengthening.[38]

Courageous conversations are not always comfortable. That doesn't mean they should be avoided. One of my board members, Cathy Taylor, reminds me of this constantly: not every conversation that needs to be had will be fun, but they still need to be had. She is brilliant at being direct, clear, and sincere with what needs to be said. Without over-justifying it. And then she is quiet.

For me, it used to be difficult to tell employees that they were not doing their best work. Even though I may want to avoid such conversations, I've learned through years of experience running a company that holding back does not allow for the company and its employees to grow and prosper together. When framed in a constructive and sincere manner, such discussions can actually boost the person's desire to improve. Plus, I have the opportunity to learn and connect with the person in a way that inspires me to be a better employer. Courageous conversations are a two-way exchange, where both people gain as they foster the relationship. That's the beauty behind it!

POWER MOVE

Make a list of all the courageous conversations that deep down you know you should have but have been putting off.

Business:
Coworker:
Friend:
Spouse/partner:
Family member:

Courageous conversations can also be simple ones like canceling a dinner engagement or meeting. When we hold back from sharing bad news or a change of plans because we don't want to disappoint, we can make matters worse for others and ourselves. Try your best to deliver disappointing news promptly, but it's okay to dispense good news over time. As soon as you know you have a conflict that prevents you from being at the engagement, let the other party know. Get the guilt out of your head, be mindful of everyone's time, and let them move on and make alternate plans. By taking personal responsibility and speaking up, you free the space for everyone involved to move forward in a positive way.

The best and only way to have a calm courageous conversation is to approach it with mindfulness, and with both our ears *and* hearts listening. It can also help to keep emotions in check. Listening with our hearts doesn't mean becoming emotionally attached or defensive, and taking comments personally as a result. Listening with our hearts means listening deeply, openly, and without judgment—to come into the conversation from a place of kindness.

The best and only way to have a calm courageous conversation is to approach it with mindfulness, and with both our ears and hearts listening.

At some point you may need to have a courageous conversation to inform someone that you're in love with them. In that case, let the genuine emotions flow! When love is on the line, and to move the relationship forward, you surrender to the love you feel and the desire to express it. I have tried it both ways, in the past choosing to keep my feelings of love close to the chest, as I didn't want to risk being hurt. I will tell you, though, that keeping my feelings a secret did not draw love closer to me. Like attracts like. If you love, show it. It will only bring love closer to you. Be the love you want to receive back in your life. So many of us walk around afraid of being hurt, so we don't express in words what we really need to say. Protecting ourselves from courageously expressing love doesn't bring love, and it can hurt others who wanted to feel loved by us.

POWER MOVE

My Favorite Conversation Tips

- *Enter into a courageous conversation mindfully and calmly.*

- *Set an intention for the conversation: What do I want to accomplish with this conversation? Knowing your intention before engaging in conversation can help you stay above the emotion.*

- *Visualize the outcome you desire.*

- *Remain flexible and open to new information.*

- *Remember, it's not about winning or losing. It's all about fostering relationships and constructive dialogue. And like exercising a muscle, it could be uncomfortable and difficult at first, but the more you practice, the better you will be at it.*

Although you have your goal in mind, I find my best outcomes come when I remain flexible to new ideas that arise from the conversation. If you learn something new that is upsetting, or gives you a completely different perspective, it is sometimes helpful to tell the other person you need to take a moment before getting back to them. If the new information causes you momentary confusion or mixed feelings, the best thing you can do is to step away and give yourself time to consider.

> Whatever words we utter should be chosen with care for people will hear them and be influenced by them for good or ill.
> *Dwight Goddard*

Own your words. They hold so much power! Like attracts like. Remember:

- Speak and write only what you want reflected back to you in life.
- Ask for help! But, whether it's with your voice or through an email, choose your words wisely when asking.
- Talk about your goals and intentions in action mode and in present tense.
- Speak positively about yourself.
- Have courageous conversations frequently.

You are in the process of doing great things in life so let your words reflect this. It makes a big impact on the energy you give off and that which comes back to you. Put out positive vibes to get positivity back!

THE POWER OF BEING READY AND FEARLESS

There is only one thing that makes a
dream impossible to achieve:
the fear of failure.

Paulo Coelho, *The Alchemist*

've given you a lot of tools to consider in this book so far, the same
tools that helped me move past my limiting beliefs and behaviors
and enter into a life of fulfillment, abundance, and love; they are
the same tools that I still use today. Regular practice is imperative. It

gives you the power to be ready when opportunity comes your way! As it most definitely will.

Realizing your deepest desires in life requires hard work, dedication, and continual practice. Not every moment of it will be pleasurable; there will be times when you will have to gather up the energy and give yourself a pep talk. There will even be days when you feel like you're burning the candle at both ends. But, if you're on the right path for yourself, the majority of it should feel gratifying. Because when you are in the process of doing what you love, or embarking on your path toward what you love, it will mostly feel exhilarating and inspiring to do the work!

Susan Feldman described the early days of One Kings Lane, which she started with Alison Pincus:

I had never worked as hard as we worked those first two years on One Kings Lane, but I loved every minute of it. I was completely consumed. I would wake up at 4:30 AM, send out emails, work out at 5:00 AM for an hour, shower, eat breakfast, and then sit at my desk all day long until late at night. I never even noticed the time. I was so inspired and energized. I knew I should be tired, but having my dream become a reality supercharged me. We did whatever it took to get the job done. It wasn't a question of it's not my job—if you could do it you did it."[39]

The powers you have learned so far—of personal responsibility, dreaming big, your mind, vision boards, intentions and stepping-stones, and your words—are the foundational tools to being prepared when opportunities arise. This is critical. On a few occasions I've been in the right place at the right time for a dream of mine to be realized, but I hadn't yet done the work needed to be able to seize that opportunity, so it was wasted. Well, not necessarily wasted, since times like that can be great motivators to actually do the work so that when the opportunity arises the next time, you're primed and ready. It's easy to lose patience or allow distractions to take hold when your dream feels so big or so far off in the distance. It can feel like it's not worth spending time on now. But if you have strong goals and intentions for your life, it is definitely worth the prep time now.

I was reminded of the importance of patience and practice when I read about now-famous author J. K. Rowling. If you don't know her personal story, you've probably heard of her children's fantasy series based on the character Harry Potter. Well, her story of how she started is inspiring, and it's a wonderful example of dedication and patience. Rowling came up with the idea for a young wizard named Harry Potter while delayed on a train in 1990. During the next five years she outlined her Harry Potter stories, mostly in longhand. As the years went by, she married and taught English as a second language. Post-divorce, and now with a young daughter, in 1993 Rowling found herself briefly unemployed and on government assistance. She then resolutely trained as a teacher and began teaching within schools in Scotland, all the while taking advantage of every spare minute to make progress on her story. She wrote. And wrote. And wrote. Intently and patiently.

In 1995 Rowling finished her manuscript and sent it to publishers, only to be rejected. Repeatedly. But finally a literary agent took a chance, and in 1997 Rowling's first book was published. Before long it was a smash success. Ultimately her seven-book series about Harry Potter, and the movies based upon them, were much lauded, broke publishing records, and netted her tremendous financial rewards. Through all the doubt, fear, overwhelmingness, and struggle, Rowling didn't give up on her dream to be an author. And what a mark she made in our culture with the Harry Potter books! She kept at it for five years, not knowing if she would ever be published. That's absolute dedication to a dream.

> It is our choices, Harry, that show
> what we truly are, far more
> than our abilities.
> J. K. Rowling, *Harry Potter and the Chamber of Secrets*

In addition to staying dedicated to and focused on your passion, it's helpful to purposely put yourself in the right place to be noticed by someone who could help you move forward with your dream. I just love watching former Costco executive Ginnie Roeglin, now CEO of Influence Marketing, at work. At meetings and conferences, she is always in the front row. Every single time. For many, the front row can seem like a scary place to be. It is much easier to hide in the shadows of the back row, but she warns against doing so:

You should always sit in the front row! It's a practice I've had since college. You can't fool around in the front row, and it forces you to stay engaged and make eye contact. It ensures that the professor, or the person leading the meeting, notices you.

It isn't always comfortable to sit in the front row, and some may find it frightening to expose yourself to the potential scrutiny of both your peers and your teacher, but this boldness builds resilience. If you don't take a risk, you won't learn anything new.[40]

When I asked Ginnie why she thinks women shy away from the front row she replied, "It can be a lack of confidence. It's much more comfortable to sit on the sidelines or in the shadows, but get out of your comfort zone. Get used to feeling uncomfortable. It builds resilience, and gets you noticed for the confident person that you are![41]

Sitting in the front row can take many forms. Where might you be hiding on the sidelines? Where do you need to make yourself more visible? Could this be a necessary stepping-stone for you to add to your list?

Remember, if you take the time to identify each of your intentions and stepping-stones, you can more clearly see a path. You're breaking your dream down into small, manageable, actionable pieces. By doing this you are actively changing your life right now. With each intention and stepping-stone you check off, there comes a sense of accomplishment. It is an inspiring feeling to be in the process of achieving your goal. Be primed and ready to seize your opportunity when it comes about—at the right time.

What's Holding Back Your Opportunity?

At this pivotal juncture of our transformational journey, when we've been practicing and putting in the time and prep work in order to take our final big leap, we can tend to stop ourselves. We hit the brakes. We're so close, yet we keep ourselves from crossing the finish line. As for an athlete running a marathon, the last mile is the most challenging. That's when you need to refocus and believe in your power to make your dream race happen! With our goals, however, this last-mile effect can show up through distractions and self-sabotaging behaviors, the most common ones being procrastination and fear, especially fears of unworthiness and failure.

Giving Up Procrastination

Over lunch once, a person I was mentoring labeled herself a procrastinator. She believed procrastination was essentially a permanent part of her genetic makeup, and that she could do nothing about it. What she did not realize is that procrastination is a choice! No one is born a procrastinator. Think about this. Is your dream actually what your parents want for you? Is your friend going after something that appears to be remarkable, so you're trying to be *remarkable* too? If your dream isn't authentically your own, then the behavior of procrastination can easily emerge.

When you're feeling stuck in procrastination, it's time to have a one-on-one courageous conversation with yourself, with your heart.

If you reevaluate and come to the realization that you aren't going after your personal version of a fulfilled life, and that instead you're just going through the motions out of obligation or guilt, you will be more likely to self-sabotage and procrastinate. Because deep down, you know you're not honestly going for what you desire, so what is there to motivate you to achieve it? When you're feeling stuck in procrastination, it's time to have a one-on-one courageous conversation with yourself, with your heart. Take a step back and ask yourself: *Am I really going after a dream I want? Or have I gone down a path of doing something I feel I am supposed to do?*

Moments of procrastination are good points in life to step back and reevaluate the path you're on in the first place. Is the path you're on really what inspires you? Does it feel like your calling? Or are you just hesitant to proceed because you are unsure of the outcome? Pay attention to your intuition in cases of procrastination. Remember that stepping-stones give you the ability to try your dream on for size. Maybe this dream isn't feeling so good to you now that you're starting to live it, or maybe you're realizing that this isn't what you deeply desire.

POWER MOVE

It's time to tear down every barrier you think you have, and every limiting belief you are carrying around. Ask yourself again:

- *What would I want in life if all I had were pure potential?*

- *Is this my dream, or is it someone else's?*

Once you are clear on your goal again, you might feel the need to course-correct a bit. Take down the images from your vision board that no longer reflect your deepest desires and replace them with new images that do. Fulfillment is a journey. There is never just one way to get there. There is no one-size-fits-all guideline. That is the beauty of our world. We have humanity in common, but we vary widely from one another. And thank goodness we do! If not, we wouldn't have the rich layers and experiences in life that come about from diverse life paths.

Likewise, the path you choose in life should uniquely suit you. It shouldn't feel like a chore. Reset anytime you need to; there is no shame in this. That is why we take cars for test drives! Sometimes the ride doesn't have the same beauty as the shiny exterior. The same goes with your life goals.

If a reset is in order, identify your new stepping-stones and write them down in your Life Intentions Book, as you did the first time. Now that you're clear on what it is you truly want . . . just go! Jump in and start tackling it. But if procrastination starts to creep in again, try the following Power Move.

POWER MOVE

Make a list of all the things you're procrastinating doing. Choose the most challenging item on your procrastination list, and do that first. Even if the hardest thing on your list is something you fear, in order to move closer to your dreams of a fulfilled life and to truly soar, you must do it anyway. It helps to tackle the hardest thing first. It gets it off your mind, and out of your way. This can also apply to your regular stepping-stones and intentions list. It even helps if you apply this strategy to your personal or business to-do lists. When you do the hardest thing first, the rest will feel like a breeze, and best of all, by completing the thing you fret over, you free up your mental energy from worry and give it space for something good.

Action Conquers Fear

Procrastination can signal fear or feelings of unworthiness. Are you afraid to reach your goal, or possibly afraid of rejection or failure, and as a result are subconsciously self-sabotaging the outcome by not doing what you should be doing? Maybe deep down inside you don't feel worthy or deserving?

I hate to admit it, but this is the type of procrastination that most resonates with me. In fact, this book might not have been written had I not caught myself in the act of self-sabotaging behaviors. When I met my wonderfully supportive book publishers, all I knew was that they had published *The Secret* and *The Magic*, two of my favorite books of all time. I hardly felt worthy. I was in awe! To make matters even scarier, they asked me to send them an email to set up a time to talk. An email? Write out words to someone who was going to decide if I was capable of writing a book? What if I misspelled something? What if I used improper grammar? They would see that I was not cut out to write a book and would immediately reject me!

So I sat on that business card for over a week. It's important to know that writing a book, and having it published by a noteworthy publisher, has been a major lifelong goal of mine. Major! I have been gifted so many useful tools and advantages along my journey, and I couldn't wait to share those tools with others. Writing books has been on my vision board and part of my goals and intentions for at least ten years. Each year I would carry that dream forward. In my spare time, I was dreaming up my book *Love Coming Home*. I spent many evenings and weekends writing. I even had a full-blown book proposal drafted and ready to go! And I was accomplishing mini stepping-stones along the way during this journey: authoring a recurring national newspaper column called Ask Jennifer Adams in a few major cities across the United States, contributing editorial content to major magazine publications along the way, and writing for our company blog.

The dream I had wanted so badly, the work I had done along the way . . . and now opportunity was finally right smack-dab in front of me! I was paralyzed by fear, though at first I didn't realize it. I was masking my paralysis with the guise of being too busy. Yes, I believed I was too busy to draft a two-sentence email requesting a phone call. It was a Saturday morning and I was sitting outside wasting time browsing on the web when it hit me: *I am self-sabotaging my biggest dream of all time! What am I thinking?* If I didn't muster up the courage to send the email, I was not seizing the opportunity to get a yes from the publisher. I had nothing to lose!

I took a moment to center myself, focus on my intention, write the message, and then hit the send button! First stepping-stone, checked. And they responded! I got the meeting, which was my second stepping-stone . . . and now I am grateful to be blissfully writing my books with Beyond Words Publishing. I'm sitting here, right now, full-out living my biggest dream, and so grateful that I didn't give up during those ten years of preparation.

POWER MOVE

When facing procrastination, ask yourself:

- Am I procrastinating because I'm feeling unworthy of my dream?

- Am I afraid of rejection?

- Is my dream so big that I'm allowing it to scare me into paralysis?

More than likely one of these scenarios is the case. Get real with yourself, and get back to it!

My husband continually reminds me that "action conquers fear." There is no truer statement. As Nike's motto states: Just do it. Get yourself out there! Do the thing you fear the most. Even if you have to take a baby step and only spend five minutes on your goal, put in the five minutes! Before you know it those five minutes will turn into a dream actualized.

One person who epitomizes how action conquers fear is the courageous and talented Mia Noblet, whom I interviewed for this book. I met Mia while hiking through Sedona, Arizona. There, I ran into a group of people pulling a rope from one side of a mountain all the way across to the adjacent mountaintop. One of them was literally hanging horizontally off the side of the hill, suspended by a rope around his waist, which was being held by several of his friends. He was slowly and carefully walking horizontally along the side of the mountain, with a long and seemingly heavy rope in his hands. If any one of his friends slipped, he could have been in serious trouble

In awe, I asked them what was happening. Were they planning to rappel down the side of the mountain? A sweet young woman in the group, who wasn't holding the rope, took a moment to talk with me.

As it turns out, they were doing something much more challenging: they were going to highline. And in case you haven't heard of highlining, it's a sport that involves balancing and walking on a rope or webbing that is fixed high up in the air. These people were actually planning to walk across the rope that would soon span two cliffsides—hundreds of feet up in the air!

It turns out the young woman I spoke with that day was Mia Noblet, who currently holds the world record for walking a highline distance of 493 meters (1,617 feet)! The highest height she has walked was almost 500 meters (1,640 feet) up in the air! Can you imagine even standing on top of a building that tall and looking down? It gives me chills even thinking about it.

When I left Mia that day I couldn't shake the urge I felt to learn how she overcomes the inevitable fear that must come along with an activity like highlining. What she was doing was extraordinary, and I was intrigued. I was able to track her down, and she was gracious enough to share her thoughts on fear with me.

At age eight, Mia saw a poster about highlining, which fascinated her. A dream was born. As you would expect for most eight-year-olds, highlining was not readily accessible to her, so she put her dream on hold for years and took up figure and speed skating. The desire continued to burn inside her until she could stand it no more. She and her family lived in Canada, and she had heard there were highliners in France, so she began to build her path and gave herself a deadline. She booked a ticket to France for six months out, having never set foot on a highline. She started by buying a rope and suspending it just a foot or two off the ground between two close trees in the park. She practiced daily. Then, during her six-month self-imposed time frame, she discovered a slacklining group right there in Canada. She was ecstatic!

Before her trip to France, she was able to experience getting up on a highline two or three times in her home country. She described it to me:

> I was *so* terrified at first. I was strong; I had experienced so much physically and mentally with skating, but nothing can prepare you for the highline. At first I could stand up, but

the fear of taking my first step was so intense . . . I was paralyzed . . . I couldn't take a step, not a single step! Normally people get up on the line and they at least try to walk, but I couldn't. I was paralyzed. . . . I could feel the potential for so much more . . . so I never gave up.[42]

Mia kept trying for five more months, and what she said next is so beautiful, probably the best self-awareness about fear that I have ever heard:

What I came to realize is I was working on my mind for those five months. That's where all the work needed to be done. My body was strong enough to perform the activity, but my mind was causing the paralysis.

All the work was being done mentally; I had to commit to standing up, but I had to understand why I was afraid, and how I could change it. The fear never really left, I just had to learn how to understand it and let it go. It never goes away because your body isn't meant to walk between mountains. You have to decide to trust. You're out there. Feel the fear, understand it, accept it, let it go . . . don't let it control you . . . You have to want it enough, but not so much that you let fear get in your way. When you find that fine balance of wanting something enough but not too much . . . that's how it happens.

I started to realize that every day changes. Some days are scarier and some days not so much. If I stay in the moment, and make it about only that moment, and the line, it allows me to feel what is happening now. Highline brings you to the here and now. And that's how I overcome the fear and am able to walk."[43]

Mia's personal insights are more helpful to me than any book I have read about fear. Initially she was so afraid that it caused paralysis of her body. Yet she did the mental work for five months straight to not just overcome the fear, as the fear is still there, but to identify it, sit with it for a long time, acknowledge it, and move forward despite the fear. Mia started with mini stepping-stones, and we can do the same. She gave herself a deadline and worked at it diligently. At first she didn't succeed, but she continued on. Like Mia, no matter how much fear you have around something you deeply desire, you can overcome it!

POWER MOVE

Make a list of the goals that scare you but that deep down inside you know you still want. Give yourself a deadline. Break your goals into small, manageable stepping-stones.

- *Fear will creep in. Know that it is expected.*

- *Acknowledge the fear. Know that it is there for a reason.*

- *Challenge yourself to do one thing that scares you every day. This exercise can help you get into your fear-releasing training zone!*

Feeling fear is normal and to be expected. It only becomes problematic when we allow it to paralyze us and prevent forward movement.

> Do the one thing you think you cannot do.
> Fail at it. Try again. Do better the second
> time. The only people who never tumble are
> those who never mount the high wire."
> *Oprah Winfrey*

Get in the habit of doing things that scare you. If you have goal-related things that scare you, and that you can't logistically accomplish without advanced planning, put them on your calendar. Give yourself a deadline for making them happen.

The scary things stop feeling so scary as you become more comfortable in uncomfortable situations. You'll see the results of your efforts. Taking risks and going outside of your comfort zone is where your best life has the potential to begin. Scary does not equal bad. Remember, action conquers fear!

Something I find to be very settling is to start off each day by setting an intention for the day. What matters the most for today? We all have ever-growing to-do lists that never seem to end. Realistically, you can't tackle every single item on the list, so sometimes our necessary to-do lists can lead to feelings of guilt or unworthiness for never completing everything on the list.

Before starting on any specific task or activity, if you think about what matters the most to tackle that day, it eliminates some of the noise, and can help keep you focused. It only takes a few seconds of reflection, but I find when I do this, it keeps my attention on the important things. At the end of the day, when I look back at my intention list it is a very fulfilling feeling to see that I've checked them off, and I don't worry about the other items still sitting on the list, as I was already realistic with myself in acknowledging that those are better suited for a different day. It somehow relieves the pressure of having to do it all.

Once you have set your intention for what you want to accomplish with your day, get in the habit of always doing your scariest thing first! Tackle it, and get it out of your mind and off of your plate. I promise when you do this, you will move mountains for yourself.

When you start your day by addressing your most challenging item, you will feel a sense of accomplishment and relief once it is completed. The rest of your day might even be a breeze. When you wait until the end of the day to handle a difficult task or conversation your energy is typically at its lowest; you're tired and not in your optimum state.

Use your valuable morning time to tackle the tough stuff when you are alert and as full of energy as possible. Clear that item out of your head. If you don't, you are pretty certain to be distracted with feelings of guilt and fear throughout the entire day. Making a habit of doing the hardest thing at the beginning of every day is a surefire way to get out of the procrastination and fear modes.

POWER MOVE

Start your day by setting an intention, and then ask yourself:

- Are the intentions or action items I've established for today tackling the tough items first? Or am I taking the easy way out?

- Have I scheduled my action items to coordinate with my energy level at given times throughout the day?

Being Fearless

Early in my process of expanding my vision and breaking down all my limiting beliefs about what I could or couldn't do, I identified Martha Stewart's career trajectory as something I admired and respected. It provided a great deal of inspiration for what I wanted out of my career, so it was a huge moment when I finally got the opportunity to interview Martha. Even though the interview was for the TV show I was on at the time, *The Better Show*, we got permission to film on the set of Martha's own show, in her prep kitchen! I was beyond excited.

Little did she know that I had been (ever-so-innocently) idolizing her for quite some time! Her book, *The Martha Rules*, came out at a perfect moment in my life, when I needed a little extra motivation to keep going in my business. It reminded me that she came from humble beginnings and accomplished the unimaginable. It gave me reason to believe that I, too, could accomplish some unimaginables in my life.

I was so nervous on my way to that interview; I had major butterflies of excitement. I imagined the conversation over and over again in my mind. I joked with myself that she was going to be my new best friend! As the interview started, I was so focused that I didn't realize my foot was slipping off my barstool. And then it happened: my foot came crashing down, right on top of hers! The cameras stopped, and I promptly stood up and apologized in horror and embarrassment. I physically hurt Martha—not exactly what I had hoped for as a first impression. I was not off to a good start, but luckily she didn't kick me out.

My big question to her, and the one I was almost holding my breath to hear the answer to, was how she managed the inevitable fear that can creep in on the way to fulfilling our biggest goals. For the first split second, her response surprised me, but then suddenly it all came together. What she told me was that she doesn't get afraid. Instead, when she has an idea, she gathers up all the facts, and understands the downsides and the upsides of each undertaking. And then if she still chooses to continue down that specific path, she proceeds fearlessly. She would not allow fear to interrupt the process of making her goals and dreams come true.

That was a powerful lesson for me. It reminded me that fear can be a major stumbling block, and we absolutely have the power to move beyond it. As soon as we sense it, we need to get into the habit of acknowledging the fear and letting it go, rather than allowing it to take hold and sabotage our best lives.

Fear can also show itself in the form of guilt. Dr. Connie Mariano was on active military duty when both of her sons were born. When she was only thirty-six years old, and her sons were two and four, she got her first assignment at the White House. She described her thirties as being about raising her children while moving forward in her career. She went on to say:

> Guilt can be a fear mechanism that can bog you down and become debilitating to your process of moving forward with your most fulfilled life. It is usually because there is some-thing from society, in the back of your mind, telling you that you *have* to, or *should*, do something, when your heart is telling you something different. Don't let society do that to you. In terms of the perpetual "maternal guilt" that working moms experience, I tell moms to refuse to surrender to guilt. If you are being the best you can be in your life, then your children will benefit from a mother who is happy, healthy, and fulfilled.[44]

As both Martha and Connie shared, fear is not a reason to give up or stop going for your dream. In all likelihood, when you decide to commit and take responsibility to live your best life, everything and everyone important in your life will benefit. So when you feel insecure, guilty, or afraid, remember to follow your heart and "refuse to surrender!"

> Follow your bliss and don't be afraid,
> and doors will open where you didn't
> know they were going to be.
>
> *Joseph Campbell*

POWER MOVE

My Favorite Fear-Conquering Tips

- *Identify and recognize your fear. Move forward anyway!*

- *Don't worry about failure or rejection. Move forward anyway!*

- *Think positively, and believe.*

- *Move forward . . . and take action!*

Action will help you conquer your fear. Give it a try. It works! One stepping-stone at a time is all you have to do. Don't allow fear to be a stumbling block in the pursuit of your goals in life.

Ginnie Roeglin offered this insight into how to manage fear, setbacks, or disappointments:

People often ask, *Is there something you learned during your career that you wish you had known when you were twenty-five and just starting out?* I have a very quick response to that question: I wish I had understood the power of vulnerability. As I was growing up in my career, I felt that showing emotions and vulnerability was a sign of weakness. After all, particularly in the earlier years, I often worked mostly with men, and I felt that I had to appear strong like them and not come across like an emotional female. I felt that leaders had to always show confidence and strength. But during the last ten or so years of my career, I finally learned that showing vulnerability is perhaps one of the greatest things a woman can do. We are all vulnerable, and showing that personal side of yourself makes you more approachable and authentic to everyone around you.

I once was having lunch with a young woman that I was mentoring. She was struggling in her position at the time, and that day I was having a pretty bad day myself. Shortly before lunch, my boss called and literally yelled at me on the phone about something I did that he did not approve of. I was shaken and upset by the call, and during lunch I shared what happened and how I felt with my mentee. She immediately started to cry! She said she never would have imagined that I, too, had bad days sometimes and she was not the only one. We developed a new bond and a more meaningful, deeper relationship because she was able to relate to me as a real person. From that day forward, I began to show more of my emotions and feelings and was able to build better relationships with people, which was much more successful, fulfilling, and enjoyable. I wish I had known this from the beginning.[45]

Taking Risks

Taking risks can provoke fear, but doing so is absolutely critical to moving forward toward your goals. Small risks can be considered a form of testing. You need to continually test things out along the way to success. Do your homework ahead of time, identify your path, and start small. Make sure the risk you're taking isn't completely betting the farm. But still risk.

When Susan Feldman finally made the decision to move forward with One Kings Lane, she knew there was a level of risk, but she also knew if she didn't risk, her dream would never come to fruition. She and her husband asked themselves, *How big is the downside?* Once she established her worst-case scenario, she opted to not bet her life savings, and then set an amount they were willing to risk. So as she puts it, "I took a calculated risk. But that risk was absolutely necessary."[46]

Eventually you might have a time when you need to put it all on the line. Taking risk, although scary at times, is absolutely necessary, whether it be getting a new job, moving, committing to a relationship, or making a calculated financial investment. The sooner you get used to taking small risks, the more prepared you will be when you need to go for it and risk it all.

Ginnie Roeglin provides this perspective on taking risks, even as a parent:

> To succeed you really have to trust yourself, and have the courage to know you are doing something to help yourself and your family in the long term. Even if you have to take a few steps back in pay, or go to school, you have to get out of any situation that is making you feel trapped and unfulfilled. If you don't take a risk and get out of the situation, this unhappiness will spill over into every aspect of your life: your parenting, your relationships, and even your health."[47]

When taking a risk, assess all the relevant details but don't ignore your gut feeling on the situation. Is your gut telling you that you're just having butterflies, as this is all new territory, or is your gut telling you there is something wrong? Only you can choose to pay attention to your intuition. It's an important part of taking personal responsibility for your life. If your gut is telling you something is wrong, you must pay attention to it.

If, because you don't feel quite ready, you're hesitant to take a risk and seize an opportunity that has been presented, you might be experiencing "impostor syndrome." It runs rampant in most of us, especially women. In this scenario we never feel truly ready or truly deserving, so we hesitate to take a risk when an opportunity arises, even if it could propel us closer to our goals.

Social psychologist and Harvard professor Amy Cuddy has researched and studied impostor syndrome in depth and wrote about it in her book *Presence: Bringing Your Boldest Self to Your Biggest Challenges*. She also speaks about it in her TED Talk, "Your Body Language Shapes Who You Are," which is eye-opening and inspiring, with over 45 million views! If you need an extra confidence boost, try her "power poses" that she shares in the talk. As for impostor syndrome, she states, "Impostorism causes us to overthink and second-guess. It makes us fixate on how we think others are judging us . . . worrying that we underprepared, obsessing about what we *should* be doing . . . Impostorism steals our power and suffocates our presence. If even *you* don't believe you should be here, how will you convince anybody else?"[48]

This feeling of being an impostor never completely goes away. It just changes in intensity the more you evolve, and the more your dreams reach greater heights. It doesn't mean you aren't ready. The sooner you can recognize this as a normal feeling that most people experience, no matter how senior they may appear in their field, the easier it will be for you to recognize it in yourself and break down the limiting belief before it becomes habitual behavior. Don't let impostor syndrome steal your power and talents! Believe and know that you deserve to be your best self!

> I'm good enough; I'm smart enough. Self-affirmation is where people list their core values. These are things that really make them who they are.
>
> *Amy Cuddy*

Ginnie Roeglin shared another valuable insight about the differences in men and women as they pertain to taking risks:

Documented research has shown that men will apply for a position if they meet just 60 percent of the requirements listed on a job posting, whereas women generally don't apply unless they meet almost 100 percent of the requirements. While these percentages represent an average, this trend is quite common and reflects the tendency for women to hold themselves back due to the inherent risk of failure or disappointment.

Don't be the one who tells yourself you are not ready! If someone else thinks you are ready, then you're probably ready! If you think you're not ready, ask yourself, why? Do you need to acquire more knowledge or experience in an area, or do you qualify, and you're just scared to put yourself out there? Even if you might benefit from a few more tools under your belt, why not apply to the position now and see what happens? There will always be some excuse; you just need to find the courage to not let the doubts hold you back. This is especially true for younger women. Just remember, you're never going to be 100 percent ready, so there is no point in waiting.[49]

When you're presented with a new job, a new opportunity, or a move of any kind that is right in line with your desired life goals, don't hesitate. Seize it! You deserve it. You've been working so hard on all of your stepping-stones and this is your moment.

If the person offering you the opportunity feels you are ready, you are ready! Go for it. So much opportunity is lost to hesitation or taking too long to weigh the pros and cons. Make sure you don't get paralysis of analysis. This can cause you to lose out on an opportunity altogether. Overanalysis is frequently the culprit when I encounter someone who has a life of dissatisfaction. They tend to analyze situations to death, and they have a big aversion to risk. Lingering in this type of pattern will undoubtedly leave you right where you are in life.

The good news is that you hold the power to change this limiting behavior. Risk is okay. In fact, risk is better than okay. It is necessary to establish a comfort level for uncomfortable situations. You must get beyond your comfort zone if you want to accomplish some of your wildest dreams!

Serendipitous Moments

The Universe often sends us little surprises and gifts to help us soar. It's that luck, or that chance encounter, you stumble upon at just the right moment—just when you needed it most. These gifts are sometimes referred to as coincidences, or being in the right place at the right time. I see these special moments as serendipitous and sent from the Universe, or God, depending upon your beliefs, to give us the little lift we need, right when we need it, to help us reach our fullest potential.

Pay attention to serendipitous moments as they show up in your life. Soon you will notice they are all around you. That awareness, or gratitude, for these moments as they show up will help you fully utilize them as the gifts they are intended to be. That gratitude draws more of these spectacular moments toward you—just as you need them. Amazing.

We must do the internal work so that we are ready to take full advantage of serendipitous moments when they show up in life. You can prepare yourself now by taking the time to practice the eight powers in this book.

Take action with your intentions and stepping-stones, do the hardest things first on your to-do list each day, and practice doing something—every single day—that scares you, even if it appears to be a small but calculated risk. Slowly train yourself to feel comfortable in uncomfortable situations so you can move fearlessly toward your dreams. Always listen to your gut, and don't allow procrastination to take hold without addressing the reasons behind it. Make space for the good to flow easily into your life by cleaning up your messes and incompletes, and by dealing with any lingering resentments.

Do the work now, so you're ready at just the right moment and can take full advantage of the serendipitous moments as they flow into your life. Create your own luck!

THE POWER OF
RESILIENCY

By encouraging adaption, agility,
cooperation, connectivity, and diversity,
resilience-thinking can bring us to a
different way of being in the world, and
to a deeper engagement with it.

Andrew Zolli, *Resilience*

S o, you are practicing the tools in this book, taking time to
do the exercises and possibly more, but things just don't
seem to be going your way. You've had a setback, or maybe
two or three. Maybe you received feedback that was hard to take.

If there's one thing I've learned, it is to expect setbacks, failures, and ups and downs, as they are a normal part of the process of life. The sooner you get used to that fact, the easier it is to recover, move beyond them, and be stronger and better off on the other end.

Setbacks and failures happen to everyone, and do not mean you are doomed to a life of just scraping by, or to never feeling contentment or happiness. The individuals who appear to be the most successful—on the outside appearing to have the Midas touch, where everything they lay a hand on turns to gold—have typically endured all kinds of ups and downs.

I noted in the introduction that my dear friend and mentor Chuck Martin repeatedly reminded me, "There is no straight line to success." Chuck was arguably one of the most beautiful minds of all time and has been recognized by many as being one of Southern California's most respected businessmen. He probably influenced me more than any other person I've encountered in life.

Chuck had a way of simplifying things for me, reminding me to not let the ups and downs get to me, that it was normal to have these growing pains. Then he would turn the negative into a learning opportunity. He would ask questions, knowing that quite possibly I had the answers inside of me already, getting me right back into solution mode. He'd urge me to put a plan together that would move me beyond the setback and onto an alternate path that could lead to far greater success.

After asking me to pause for a moment, Chuck would suggest that I take an honest look at each commitment I was making, to determine whether it would forward my purpose-driven life or cause distraction and complication. Chuck showed me by example that no matter what my life brought me at that moment, I could be resilient and charge forward toward my dreams, and put my life to good use. Living it to its fullest.

Chuck knew firsthand the many obstacles life can throw at you. He lived an American rags-to-riches story, beginning life in an eight-hundred-square-foot home in Iowa, next to a junkyard and railroad track. His dad was a janitor at the post office for fifty years. When Chuck was a little boy, his dad told him that no one likes a smart boy, to sit in the back of the class and keep his hand down. So he sat in the back and kept his thoughts to himself, all the while wanting more. After graduating he borrowed $300 from his family doctor and bravely took the train all the way to Southern California to start a new life for himself. He went from living next to the junkyard to living in one of the world's most exclusive enclaves in Laguna Beach—one that he had dreamt of for years.

A role model of how to live life to the fullest, Chuck nonetheless cared about how he was affecting others and how he could contribute more to everything he was doing, right up to his death in 2017. He made every second count, whether it was through the incredible love he showed for his wife, Twyla, the books he authored as he was nearing eighty years old, the one hundred emerging-growth companies he invested in, or the hundreds of students he and his wife gave scholarships to. He was so outstanding in his desire to help others that in 2013, the University of California, Irvine, awarded him the esteemed UCI Medal, which honored individuals for their impact on the world and the university.

Shortly before his passing, Chuck wrote the book *Orange County, Inc.* It tells the story of a county's remarkable emergence from a small agricultural region after World War II, with a population of barely one hundred thousand people, into one of the nation's leading economies with a population of 32 million. It goes on to tell the story of about two hundred companies in eighteen diverse industries.

This is where the story becomes applicable to all of us. Chuck opened his book with this message:

> In writing this book I was intrigued by the common attributes of the entrepreneurs who created winning companies. I also found it interesting to observe the parallels in their pathway from startup to success; their path to success was rarely a straight line. Their journeys were seldom without challenges, and some seemed overwhelming; often the founders traveled to the edge of oblivion.[50]

If all of these two hundred entrepreneurs living in the same city went through serious ups and downs on their paths to success, then why would it be abnormal for you or me to experience setbacks too? These entrepreneurs all grew to great heights, despite unbelievable twists and turns. They all survived. And not only that, but they all flourished. Setbacks and failures are a normal part of the process of life. Not only in business, but in our personal lives as well.

Dr. Connie Mariano tells a serendipitous story about a time when her dream of becoming an OB-GYN suddenly changed course:

I became a doctor with the dream of becoming an OB-GYN specialist. I even volunteered in women's clinics as a teenager. That dream was shattered when I did my first OB-GYN rotation at a hospital during my third year in medical school. I was intimidated and bullied by a senior resident who completely turned me off to entering that field. He was verbally abusive and made me feel like a failure, like I was stupid and not cut out for the work. I was so disappointed and devastated by the experience, feeling unworthy of the career path I had worked so hard for and wanted so badly. The following month, I did my rotation in internal medicine at Walter Reed Army Hospital. The internal medicine doctors were brilliant, compassionate, and caring. I told them I wanted to be like them, so at that pivotal moment I made the decision to change direction and become a physician specializing in internal medicine.

Fast-forward thirty years later, I am the keynote speaker at the annual convention of the American College of Gynecologic Surgeons being held at a resort in Tucson, Arizona. The night before my speech, the faculty is honoring me at a dinner. I look across the table and there is a familiar name on the card; it is the same doctor who intimidated me during my third-year OB-GYN rotation. I told him I was one of his medical students, but he had no memory of me.

I told him that I would never forget him and that I would mention him in my opening remarks.

The next morning, before my presentation on presidential healthcare, I shared with the audience that I almost became an OB-GYN doctor, but a particular doctor in their group convinced me otherwise. I told them I owe my White House career to that doctor who convinced me not to go into OB-GYN and instead, I went into internal medicine, which changed the course of my career and my life.

After my presentation, and a standing ovation from the audience, as I was exiting the auditorium, I was greeted one last time by the OB-GYN doctor. He was profusely apologetic when he realized he had been so difficult to me during my medical school rotation. I told him I forgave him, and thanked him for making me change course in my career.[51]

In your journey toward making your deepest desires come true, it is critical to accept that setbacks and failures of any kind do *not* mean that you are finished or that all hope is lost. They can actually lead you directly to a path that is even better suited for you. One that is more remarkable than what you had in mind in the first place. It is so easy to go to the extreme negative when we have a down period in life. You are not alone, and you are not abnormal because of it. You are just on your way to better days!

A good part of my Harvard Business School Owner/President Management (OPM) education focused on setbacks, and even on surviving crisis. We analyzed case study after case study of noteworthy businesses and people who struggled mightily along their journeys before achieving success. Why? Because even Harvard recognizes struggle as a normal part of business and life.

It's what we do with setbacks and failures that determines our future. We can choose to bury our heads in the sand and run for the hills, or we can learn from these ups and downs and be resilient. The best part of this is that it's your choice.

Failure teaches us more than success. You often need to endure the first to enjoy the second. Take confidence in knowing you are not alone when you experience a setback or failure. It's a normal part of the process of life. You are resilient, and will be better for it. Resiliency is key.

> While resilience helps us recover from
> loss and trauma, it offers much more than
> that. True resilience fosters well-being,
> an underlying sense of happiness, love,
> and peace. Remarkably, as you internalize
> experiences of well-being, that builds
> inner strengths which in turn make
> you more resilient.
> Rick Hanson, PhD, *Resilient*

The Gift of Resiliency

Not every request will result in a yes; we all get nos along the way. I still get them. I've gotten so many nos that I can't even begin to count them! I remember going after my biggest design project to date. It was in Cabo San Lucas, and while I knew the project was a big stretch for my small team, I really felt we were ready. We were up against really big global design firms. I hardly felt worthy. When the time came to submit our proposals I got a no—a flat-out rejection. It came in written form. I was so disappointed and "ran" to one of my mentors, Eli Morgan (I mentioned him earlier in the book) for advice. He asked me, "What was their objection?" When I said I had no idea, he asked, "Well then how can we turn it to a yes?" He encouraged me to get on a plane and fly to the prospective client for a face-to-face meeting. I did, and still got a no, but I left with some powerful information. The potential client told me why they had rejected my team's proposal. Armed with this information, I went back to my mentor, and we created a list of stepping-stones that I needed to do to show the project owners and managers that I could effectively overcome every single thing that concerned them. So I tried one last time . . . and the third time was the charm. I'll never forget the feeling! I got a personal email from one of the project owners who said, "We can't get over your passion, and we respect that. And because of that respect, we are going to give you a chance!" Tears are rolling down my face just remembering that moment. So many nos, and then I finally got a yes! To this day, reflecting on that email gives me strength when I encounter setbacks and rejection. No only means not today!

Remember, every no gets you closer to a yes. No just means not today. Pause and take that in. How many times have you been told no, only to eventually turn it into a yes, possibly without even realizing it was happening?

POWER MOVE

Remember that no means just not today, and figure out how to overcome the objection for the next time.

Every time you get turned down, you gain a little bit of information that makes you stronger for the next time. If you're going after something you truly desire, don't give up on the first, second, or even third try. Keep asking.

With every no, or disappointment, ask yourself how you can make improvements, be tenacious, and be willing to work hard to regain your footing. You will eventually be able to turn that no into a yes if you do the work to overcome the objections along the way.

With every rejection, try to reflect on why you got a no. Focus on the objection that needs to be overcome so you can be stronger for it and better off the next time. There are so many powerful lessons—actually gifts—when receiving a no. Dust yourself off and keep on going. The no you received does not mean you are flawed. It just means the other person chose to not go along with what you were offering that day. Someone else will, and quite possibly that same person will be the one to accept your offer the next time you make it, after you've polished your request.

Mistakes Happen

You can strive for excellence in all you do, but please don't worry about achieving perfection. If perfection is your goal, you will continually be disappointed. By yourself and by others. When you make a mistake, remember that it's normal; it's what you do to correct the mistake that matters, so fix it and don't repeat it.

Whether you've made a poor decision, said the wrong thing, messed something up that affected you or others, missed a deadline, or fell for a lie or mistruth, know that we all make such mistakes from time to time. Learn from your setbacks. They can propel you forward.

POWER MOVE

- *If you've made a mistake that affects someone else, apologize fast.*

- *Step back and analyze what went wrong.*

- *Use the opportunity to learn so you won't make the same mistake again.*

Don't try to cover up a mistake, or even worse, shift blame to someone else. It only reflects poorly on you. There is something disarming when someone simply admits, *I messed up. I am so sorry!* What else can you really say after that? When someone takes the deserved blame and flat-out apologizes, there's not much more that needs to be said. In the aftermath of a mistake, be the person you would want someone else to be to you. Once you apologize, offer up a solution on how you will rectify the mistake. Learn from it, and then let it go!

What should you never do again? What can you do better the next time? Taking time to step back and reflect on your mistake reveals clues that can lead you to success. You're actually a leg up on someone else who hasn't made the same mistake. You have the knowledge that comes from experience in the trenches. The others who haven't yet experienced the same pitfall still have a learning curve. Your mistake, if handled properly, is a gift to you.

Personally, I have little tolerance for making the same mistake twice. When I do this, or see someone else do it, it confirms for me that we've wasted a big opportunity. Be present, take personal responsibility, and reflect on your mistakes so you can learn from them. Use mistakes as the gifts that they are.

However, I'm quite tolerant of others and myself on a first-time mistake. I have made every mistake imaginable in my company and many in my life. When I have an employee who makes a mistake and apologizes, together we can fix it, grow, and move on. My take on mistakes is that if you aren't making mistakes, you aren't pushing yourself hard enough. Try, fall down, learn, get up, and try again, grow, and succeed!

We can work like heck to avoid failure.
But the truth is, if we never fail,
it means we're really not trying
hard enough.

Michelle A. Williams

Moving on is key. It is easy to wallow in guilt, self-pity, or embarrassment. Allow yourself to feel whatever emotion you're feeling, but be resilient. Move on. Holding on to that embarrassment doesn't help the situation. Learn from it but let it go. Wallowing, rehashing, and continually beating yourself up keeps you from moving forward and applying the valuable learnings you have just experienced. I can't emphasize this point enough: *Let it go!* Free up your valuable headspace to let the good flow in.

Accepting Change

Change of any kind can feel unsettling, especially when it is thrust upon you and seems to be out of your control. Typically with change we tend to go to the worst-case scenario, feeling powerless. In the end change isn't as bad as we think it has the potential to be, and most often it opens doors to opportunities you might not have otherwise considered. Sometimes it gives us that little kick in the pants we needed anyway.

Change is inevitable. Try to find the adventure in it where you can.

I asked entrepreneur Susan Feldman for her perspective on change, and she had a great response: "You have to be flexible and open to the journey. You have to have a mind-set of *I know that's how we did things yesterday, but this is how we're doing it today.*"[52] She went on to say that a time of great change and of needing to be flexible with her role at One Kings Lane proved to be the most fun she'd ever had. That's a great thing to keep in mind. Change is inevitable. Try to find the adventure in it where you can.

I asked Glenn Stearns a similar question, and he had this perspective:

Fear and worry only mean something is about to change in your life. When we feel these feelings, it is time to embrace the inevitable fact that there will be change. Be excited and face the feelings head-on. Every growth opportunity has the potential to transform us. We just might not know it at the time. Be excited, focus, and communicate better than ever when feelings of fear and worry enter our minds. It just may be the opportunity we needed but didn't see coming.[53]

Change most definitely can bring about good things. It helps to keep this perspective, especially when the change is unwelcome.

When change happens that is not your choice it's extra valuable to have the tools in this book. Go back to your vision board. What is it that you wanted for yourself in the first place? Get yourself back into the driver's seat, readjust your path if need be, and go after your dream anew. Look for the gifts that have occurred from the change. If it's a lost job, for example, that job probably wasn't quite right for you in the first place. What type of job do you sincerely want?

It can be unsettling to have something decided for you that you feel you had no say in, but it can be a major gift if you use it to reposition yourself toward something you want even more. Sometimes it's good to be forced out of your comfort zone. If at all possible, try not to commit to something out of panic or insecurity. It's so easy to do in these types of circumstances. Possibly you will have to fill in a financial gap temporarily, but keep your chin up, and *know* it is only temporary.

Sometimes it can feel like it's all too much, that it would be easier to throw in the towel. Believe me, I still have those days, even those weeks, but through practicing all of the eight powers in this book, I can get back on track much faster than ever before. When I'm feeling this way about unexpected or undesired change, I let myself feel the feelings, as I now realize they will eventually pass.

In these tough moments, go back to expanding your vision, *What would I want if I knew I could not fail?* I have asked myself this question for years, especially in times of disappointment, or if I'm just feeling off, in general. Feeling off can signal that you're out of sync with your core values and deepest desires. I re-ask myself, *If I broke down every limiting belief about myself and my current circumstance, what would I really want?*

Then go to your vision board. Sometimes I adjust any images I feel are no longer relevant, and I put up new ones that feel more inspiring. But more often than not, I realize that I am experiencing growing pains—setbacks and frustrations that are bound to occur as I'm charting new territory for myself and my company. Having never experienced this new territory before, how could I have all the answers at the onset? I am bound to make mistakes, hit roadblocks, and become exhausted.

Growing pains should not cause you panic. Take time for deep reflection and slight course corrections. Everyone experiences growing pains in one way or another, and you, too, will get through them.

During such times it can be helpful to seek out a mentor who has been in a similar situation. This is the time to be especially careful who you ask for advice. Growing pains are critical for growth, and when addressed and properly cared for, they can offer big rewards. The good news is this uncharted territory signals that you are growing!

Here are some of my favorite ways to get back on track and return to a positive mind-set: make the mental shift to gratitude, get out of your own head, acknowledge your successes, and remember that circumstances change.

Switch to Gratitude

When you're feeling discouraged, go to gratitude. Looking at the positive helps immensely during times of frustration or worry. Look at all that your current path has brought you, and look beyond your current dream path too. Shift to gratitude in all aspects of your life.

> Joy is what happens when we
> allow ourselves to recognize
> how good things are.
> *Marianne Williamson*

Write down everything you can think of to be grateful for. Realize that you are on the path to satisfying your deepest desire, and that not every part of the journey is meant to be easy. Be grateful for what you have, and you will not only attract more of it but also feel happier.

In 2011, a study was conducted in which individuals wrote and delivered letters in which they expressed gratitude for the intended recipient. Reportedly, the letter writers experienced elevated happiness and greater life satisfaction, even weeks after the task was completed. "In the pursuit of happiness and life satisfaction, gratitude is showing a direct and long-lasting effect thus the more gratitude we experience the happier our lives will be."[54]

Gratitude works as an instant pick-me-up with far-reaching benefits. If you are feeling low, go to gratitude . . . over and over again, if necessary. Disrupt your current mind-set and reset it with gratitude.

Getting Out of Your Own Head

Think back to a time when you helped someone or aided in a cause of some kind. Didn't you receive more than you gave? One of the things that helped me the most during my painful divorce was giving my time to a local charity in Portland, Oregon, called Self Enhancement, Inc. It got me out of my head and helped me to realize just how great a life I have. Being around others, being of service, is not only doing good for others but also doing good for yourself.

It is hard to stay in your own negative headspace when you are helping someone. Even though the motivation is to aid the other person, you are also disrupting your fixation and shifting your focus to compassion and service. Remember we talked about quieting our minds? This is one way to do just that. It quiets your own thought patterns and refocuses your energy. I promise this will help you get just the reset you need.

The next time you encounter individuals engaged in giving back, look at their faces. There will pretty much always be a beautiful smile. I was hiking the other day and was suddenly overcome with joy—in fact I'm smiling now just thinking of it. There was a small group of five volunteers with shovels in their hands, doing hard manual labor digging to make the trail more enjoyable for others. Despite the hard work in the hot Arizona sun, there was laughter, smiles, and joy radiating from each of them.

One of my friends and employees, Susan Smalley, has experienced a life journey that is both tragic and inspirational. Sadly, she lost the love of her life, her husband, to a sudden heart attack. And years later, when she finally had the courage to move on, she lost her long-standing boyfriend the same way. Susan sets the best example of resiliency of anyone I've seen. She pours her energy into giving back. She chairs an organization that helps disabled children and young adults, called Arizona Magic of Music and Dance, and she volunteers weekly at an animal shelter, even choosing to start work earlier on Mondays so she can walk dogs in need in the afternoons. She looks for every opportunity to do a random act of kindness for someone.

One day a woman contacted our office in hopes of getting a smaller blanket to take with her to her chemo treatments. Susan took it upon herself to cut and sew a blanket we had on site and swiftly get it out the door so this woman could feel comfortable during her treatments. Susan has every reason to be sad, and she battles with grief every day, but she intentionally chooses to disrupt that mind-set by helping others instead of feeling sorry for herself. She is our shining office angel who makes everyone feel good by the example she sets for all of us.

You don't have to undertake a massive charity endeavor to do good and quiet your mind. Look for random ways to make someone's day a little better. Simple random acts of kindness are an easy way to help you move beyond a challenging time in your life, or a negative mind-set. They are also experiences that connect us to others, cultivating compassion and empathy.

Acknowledge the Successes

Another good trick to get yourself back to feeling positive is to go through your vision board images that have come true. This can give you the renewed confidence to realize you have achieved success in the past, so you can do it again! Reflect on those successes. No matter how big or small the accomplished goals are, this review and reflection is uplifting and empowering. Remember the work it took to get you there, the worry and setbacks you had along the way, and the sweet feeling of accomplishment once your desire came to fruition. Do that over and over with every image. It is a powerful pick-me-up.

Dig even deeper, if needed. Go to past successes that you had as a child, as a teenager, or in your early twenties. Think about each chapter in your life and something that you accomplished during it.

This can help you realize that you have overcome difficulties in the past, and you can surely overcome them now that you have more years, wisdom, and tools under your belt.

Ahead of a crisis or setback, listing mini life successes and filing them away where they're easily accessible can be a powerful resource for you in times of need. It is a good way to acknowledge the things you've done right, the challenges you have overcome. It will remind you how resilient you are.

Remember That Circumstances Change

I once cosigned for a loan, and the other party defaulted. I thought my financial life was over. Not just my financial life, but my entire life! For almost a year, I had to make the other person's payments. I was so bitter, so resentful, it ate me alive! One day as I was ranting and raving about the situation to one of my dear friends, Al Fleenor, he said to me, "Life has an uncanny way of working itself out." That's all he said about my problem. It was definitely not what I wanted to hear at that moment, as I did not think it applied to my situation; in my mind, my setback was insurmountable. But come to find out he was right. It wasn't a year later that the person was miraculously able to repay the loan to the bank, and even made me whole on my payments. Overnight my problem was gone, when for over a year I saw no way out. As I reflect on it, it seems like a bump in the road, one I struggle to remember clearly now, but at the time it felt debilitating.

In times of great stress, find solace in remembering that life has an uncanny way of working itself out. Solidify this knowledge by reflecting on past obstacles you've overcome and realizing that you are powerful beyond belief. Life will work itself out.

Whatever you are stressed about right now, you probably had something else you were equally as stressed about a year ago, and are barely able to remember today. If you do remember it, maybe you're chuckling to yourself, *Oh, yeah, that . . . I can't believe how much I worried over that, and yeah, it's all just fine now!*

I asked world record–holding highliner Mia Noblet how she deals with the inevitable setbacks she experiences, as she encounters so many diverse situations: weather conditions, the way she is feeling on any given day, and many other unknowns as she continues to grow her unique highlining dream. Her mind-set is truly the one we need:

Part of me is just very patient with myself, and I know the potential is there. Many get so frustrated, and give up, but I'm always happy and grateful to be out there on the line, no matter how hard it might be that day. I'm okay with wherever I am, and however well I did that day. I never view things as a setback. If it doesn't happen, there is another day and another time. Keep trying. You try something and sometimes it doesn't work, and sometimes it does. I never take it negatively, I just realize that my goal was not fully achieved today, and that's okay, I'm happy with what I achieved today.[55]

200

In times of great stress, find solace in remembering that life has an uncanny way of working itself out. Solidify this knowledge by reflecting on past obstacles you've overcome and realizing that you are powerful beyond belief. Life will work itself out.

Remember that tomorrow is a new day!

Conclusion:
Let Your
Light Shine

Life is no "brief candle" for me.
It is a sort of splendid torch, which I
have got hold of for the moment;
and I want to make it burn as
brightly as possible before handing it
on to future generations.

George Bernard Shaw

What makes your heart soar? What dreams burn deeply inside of you? Whatever your answer is, you must go after it! Even if at first it seems like you are going against the norm, or that there is no way of making your dream a reality, trust me, there is a way to bring it to life. It will require patience, hard work, and dedication, but it is so worthwhile—not just achieving the goal but also the journey itself is incredibly enriching.

Starting your journey with baby steps is fine. Once you start on your path, you unleash a lot of power. And as you move forward, your dreams will expand and you will evolve as a human being, so remember that it's a lifelong endeavor that never ends. Take the time you need. There is no race to reach the top or prove anything to any-one—it's your journey—you're living your best and most authentic life.

After I first identified my goal of launching a bedding line, it took several years of research to learn how I could make it hap-pen. Even though at times I would get discouraged, wondering if I would ever be able to launch the line, the inspiration that came as a result of the process was a delight! I was exploring and learning; my awareness of all the possibilities for how to make my dream happen were unfolding right in front of me.

I had to remind myself to be patient and persistent while I pur-sued my big dream and simultaneously ran my design business— the daily tasks and responsibilities that I didn't necessarily love but had to do. Maybe this is true for you too. Whether your dream is to move to another city, travel abroad, find a new love, be of ser-vice, or learn a new hobby, it will undoubtedly take time, focus, and planning.

When the research and planning phase was over and I was ready to launch my bedding line, I realized I had limited funds to invest in the undertaking. I identified $5,000 that I could risk, so I needed to start extremely small and be resourceful. Instead of renting a warehouse space to store the bedding items, my personal design office turned into my receiving dock and warehouse. And then, with each online order that came in, I was the fulfillment and packing person. I couldn't afford to hire help, so it was my responsibility to make sure each order was handled and executed from beginning to end. Reflecting on times like this, I'm reminded that we all have to start somewhere; Apple founder Steve Jobs started his venture in his parents' garage!

So try not to be too hard on yourself, or to compare your progress to others who appear to be further ahead. We may not know the whole story, or what challenges they may or may not have faced along the way. With patience, hard work, and dedication, you will get there. Use others you respect as sources of inspiration for what's possible, but don't let it knock you off your own path. Never in a million years would I have believed that my small bedding line would grow into an international business, one that has evolved into a multitude of other home furnishings products, too!

Kim Brown, someone I met through shared speaking engagements geared toward empowering other women, is another person who stayed determined and patient in order to realize her big dream. Kim came from humble beginnings. Being raised by a single father, she had to start working at the age of twelve, as her family needed the money. On top of that she also had to help raise her three younger siblings. At one point, they so desperately needed money that Kim thought it was a better use of her time to drop out of high school and accept a management position at McDonalds. She quickly realized the error in that decision, and identified a way to keep her job and re-enroll in school. But Kim longed for more. She didn't want to live from paycheck to paycheck, she wanted a life that fulfilled her. Through self-reflection, she identified higher education as a positive pathway, and going to college became her big dream.

In fact, Kim wanted it so badly that she decided to start living her dream right then and there. She enrolled in college while she was in high school! It took Kim ten years to get her bachelor's degree, and understandably so. She was finishing high school, at times working full time, and then shortly after high school she became a young mother of two. She says this of her journey:

> It was tough, but I knew it was the stepping-stone I needed to have my dream of options and financial freedom come true. I wanted this for myself, and also eventually for my children. I wanted to be able to look back and tell them that I had the courage to go after my dream in hope of someday being an inspiration to them. This desire kept me inspired. I was so tired, and I made sacrifices along the way, but the reward was worth it. I feel great joy in knowing I did something all of those years ago that I now thank myself for. I feel free because I pursued and achieved my dream! I now have the option to pursue the other dreams I want in my life.
>
> Now, in times of setback or inevitable disappointments, I look back and think, how in the world did I do all of that? Knowing I accomplished what I set in my mind gives me the strength to keep going no matter what adversity I might be facing at the moment. I now know there is not much that I can't take on. I proved that to myself.

We can tend to get derailed or discouraged when things get tough, but to think we can ever achieve something big without some type of struggle is kidding ourselves. If you're going to achieve anything, you have to be able to handle the tough times. Realize that once you set a goal for yourself, even it if takes twenty years, you can get there. Chip away, every day, every month. Do everything in your life with intention—the intention of reaching the goal you have set for yourself. That is how you make your dreams come true. You can do what you set your mind to. You have to stay focused. The payoff is freedom. The financial security is nice, but the freedom that comes from living the life you want is the ultimate reward![56]

Wherever you are today, know that whatever you want, it is within your capability and your reach. Like Kim, you just need to go after it. You need to begin. Take flight and soar!

The eight powers in this book will lift you to your fullest potential, giving you wings that will help you to take flight and soar.

You are now equipped with eight powerful tools that, when used together, can bring about extraordinary things in your life. No matter what it is you yearn for—an adventure, a career, an artistic or athletic challenge, a savings account, a partnership, a family, deeper friendships, higher education, or a new place to live—when you apply all of these tools together you unleash a force within yourself that has actually been there all along! The eight powers in this book will lift you to your fullest potential, giving you wings that will help you to take flight and soar.

Take Action Now! I promise you will thank yourself for it later. Don't look back and think, *I wish I had started a year ago.* Start right now. Your dream life is your personal responsibility. Go after it!

Identify Your Wildest Dreams! Breakdown every limiting belief, and every current circumstance in your life, and dream with reckless abandon. What do you want out of life? You must take pause to identify and get clear on what this is for you.

Create Your Stepping-Stones: This becomes your how. It's your path to your most fulfilled life. Don't allow them to live in your head, though. You must get your stepping-stones out on paper. This is your To Do list for life.

Use Your Vision Board: Put it in places where you can easily view and access it every single day. And then, as John Assaraf says, "get off your ass and make it happen!" If the images were possible for someone, then why not you?

Harness the Power of Your Mind: Visualize exactly what you want. Your mind is an incredibly powerful tool. Replay your desired result in your mind. See your dream fulfilled. And when you need to reset and refresh, quiet your mind to allow the creativity and breakthroughs to flow.

Choose Your Words Mindfully: Both when talking and writing about your dreams. Say them in the present and in action mode. And you absolutely must ask for what you want. You are brave. Reflect this in your words.

Fear is ok! It will come and go, and that's natural. Let it in. Acknowledge it . . . and then release it. Take some risks. There is no fun in playing it safe. Fearlessly and unabashedly go after your dreams. You deserve this.

Resilient You! We all have our off days, our mistakes and setbacks. They are not special to only you. Pick yourself back up! Onward and upward. Your dreams still await! You are just as deserving and capable as anyone else.

Look for moments of serendipity. I see my sister Erica in every butterfly that flutters by me. Butterflies lend me courage. She sends them to me when I need support. When I first set up a design office in San Diego, in addition to the office I had in Portland, Oregon, I was very nervous. It was a risk and a big undertaking. Yet San Diego was something I had wanted ever since my family and I embarked on that long childhood road trip to see my aunt. I had taken all the risks into account, made a plan, found a tiny office space . . . and launched! But, quite frankly, I was still feeling apprehensive and scared, thinking, *What if this move puts me out of business completely? What if this is something I can't manage?*

When I opened my new office, I started noticing butterflies outside my front door. It was magical. They were everywhere! Come to find out from a neighboring tenant, the butterflies had been cocooning right underneath my awning for years. In fact, she would remind the cleaning crew to avoid disturbing the area, so that the butterflies could flourish. And this loveliness was now a part of my office space!

I had front-row seats to this spectacular show of seeing former caterpillars come out of their cocoons and metamorphose into their full potential as butterflies! Every season they would repeat this cycle of transformation before my eyes. What a coincidence . . . or maybe not! I believe it was my sister bringing this good fortune to me. It gave me the immediate confidence that despite the risk I was taking, I was doing exactly what I needed to do . . . and that everything would be fine. And it was.

Find your butterflies. Find the things that lift you, that give you a boost.

Find your butterflies. Find the things that lift you, that give you a boost. They could come in the form of mentors, supportive friends, or even objects or places that give you special energy, like crystals, plants, or the beach. It could be prayer or meditation. It could be your inspiring vision board that creates magic in your life. Look to your past successes. Remind yourself that you deserve the life that you are going after just as much as anyone else does.

Setbacks will happen. Expect them. That way when they arise, they don't come as a surprise. You will have times when setbacks, disappointments, or constructive feedback you receive can get you down. Believe me, I know! Acknowledge the feeling of disappointment, but then let your resilient self emerge and keep moving forward. Learn from each situation and be better for it. Use the resiliency tools in this book. Though setbacks might temporarily hold you down, know that this is a temporary situation. Use them as a launching opportunity to soar. Recover and take flight once more!

Most importantly, let your light shine bright. Embody joy, grace, and kindness. And above all, be grateful! Like attracts like. Be the light you want reflected back to you.

What are your biggest, boldest, wildest dreams? What would you do if you knew all you had was pure potential? Continually ask yourself this throughout your life journey. And then begin! So much joy and fulfillment is out there waiting for you. Get started!

All our dreams can come true, if we have the courage to pursue them.
Walt Disney

Acknowledgments

I am extremely grateful to my publishers, Richard Cohn and Michele Ashtiani Cohn, for gifting me the pathway to see one of my biggest dreams come true. Thank you for having faith in me and for seeing the potential of this book. You continually lifted me up throughout this emotional journey so I could soar and continue on with my writing. You gave me the wings I needed every step of the way.

Thank you to Emily Han, my editor and guiding star throughout the writing process. You offered me great insight and perspective into how to harness my stories, organize my thoughts, and ultimately create a book others would enjoy reading. I could not have done this without you.

To Lindsay Brown and the entire design and copyediting team at Beyond Words, I greatly appreciate your tireless attention to detail! I especially loved when you created vision boards of inspiring ideas for what my book's cover could become. You expanded my vision of possibilities. Until I met you, I had no idea how many layers of work go into bringing a book to life.

To Katie Meyers, my diligent research assistant: you are the beautiful bonus I received when I married your dad. It brought me so much joy to work with you on this book. You were brilliant at digging up data, facts, and quotes when I needed them most. Thank you for the late nights and long weekends spent helping me!

I feel deep gratitude toward my many contributors to this book. Thank you, especially, to Mia Noblet, Ginnie Roeglin, Glenn Stearns, Susan Feldman, JR Meyers, John Assaraf, Connie Mariano, Eli Morgan, Cindy Mulflur, Kim Brown, and Susan Smalley. You opened up and showed vulnerability so that others could benefit from your words of wisdom.

And last but definitely not least, thank you to my patient, loving husband for your never-ending support and for helping me forward in my dream! You even did extra work around the house so I could write with fewer distractions. I would trade writing for household chores any day, so I'm glad you perfected that skill set (wink!). Thank you for being the inspiration when I needed it and the shoulder to cry on as I experienced great waves of emotion. You are everything I had on my vision board—and so much more. I love you!

Bonus Resources for Soaring

The following resources (some of my favorites!) have helped me along my journey:

Books

The Secret by Rhonda Byrne

The Magic by Rhonda Byrne

The Success Principles: How to Get from Where You Are to Where You Want to Be by Jack Canfield

Innercise: The New Science to Unlock Your Brain's Hidden Power by John Assaraf

Inspiration: Your Ultimate Calling by Wayne W. Dyer

The Greatest Salesman in the World by Og Mandino

The Power of Positive Thinking by Norman Vincent Peale

The Complete Vision Board Kit: Using the Power of Intention and Visualization to Achieve Your Dreams by John Assaraf

Change Your Thoughts, Change Your Life: Living the Wisdom of the Tao by Wayne W. Dyer

The 7 Habits of Highly Successful People: Powerful Lessons in Personal Change by Stephen R. Covey

Harvard Business Review magazine

Coach Wooden's Leadership Game Plan for Success: 12 Lessons for Extraordinary Performance and Personal Excellence by John Wooden and Steve Jamison

Meditation Apps and Programs*

Deepak Chopra and Oprah Winfrey's 21-Day Meditation Experience

Headspace

Insight Timer

Holosync†

Calm

* Many of the apps below are subscription based.

† Available only for iPhones.

Notes

1. Rhonda Bryne, *The Secret* (New York: Atria Books/Beyond Words, 2006), 151.

2. Eckhart Tolle, *The Power of Now: A Guide to Spiritual Enlightenment* (Sydney, Australia: Hachette, 2008), Kindle edition, chap. 4, "Wherever You Are, Be There Totally."

3. Randy Pausch, *The Last Lecture* (New York: Hyperion, 2008), 17.

4. Manoush Zomorodi, *Bored and Brilliant: How Spacing Out Can Unlock Your Most Productive and Creative Self* (New York: St. Martin's Press, 2017), 3.

5. Eva Selhub, "Nutritional Psychiatry: Your Brain on Food," *Harvard Health Blog*, November 17, 2015, https://www.health.harvard.edu /blog/nutritional-psychiatry-your-brain-on-food-201511168626.

6. Marianne Williamson, *A Return to Love: Reflections on the Principles of "A Course in Miracles"* (San Francisco: HarperOne, 1996), 190.

7. Ginnie Roeglin (CEO, Influence Marketing, LLC), in discussion with the author, February 2018.

8. Roeglin, discussion

9. Roeglin, discussion.

10. Susan Feldman (cofounder, One Kings Lane), in discussion with the author, February 2018.

11. Dr. Connie Mariano, in discussion with the author, February 2018.

12. Anthony Robbins (@TonyRobbins), "Whatever you hold in your mind on a consistent basis is exactly what you will experience in your life," Twitter, August 28, 2015, 7:10 AM, https://twitter.com/Tony Robbins/status/637266065391681536.

13. Nathan Furr, "How Failure Taught Edison to Repeatedly Innovate," *Forbes*, June 9, 2011, https://www.forbes.com/sites /nathanfurr/2011/06/09/how-failure-taught-edison-to-repeatedly -innovate/#44b5182b65e9.

14. AJ Adams, "Seeing Is Believing: The Power of Visualization," *Flourish* (blog), *Psychology Today*, December 3, 2009, https://www .psychology today.com/blog/flourish/200912/seeing-is-believing -the-power-visualization.

15. Anna Williams, "8 Successful People Who Use the Power of Visualization," MindBodyGreen, July 8, 2015, https://www .mindbodygreen.com/0-20630/8-successful-people-who-use-the -power-of-visualization.html.

16. Jack Nicklaus (@jacknicklaus), "I never hit a shot, not even in prac- tice, without having a very sharp, in-focus picture of it in my head," Twitter, April 5, 2016, 6:16 PM, https://twitter.com/jacknicklaus /status/717521375934738432.

17. Martin E. P. Seligman, *Authentic Happiness: Using the New Positive Psychology to Realize Your Potential for Lasting Fulfillment* (New York: Free Press, 2002), 39.

18. Jack Canfield, *The Success Principles: How to Get from Where You Are to Where You Want to Be*, 10th Anniversary Edition (New York: HarperCollins, 2015), 250.

19. Wayne W. Dyer, *Getting in the Gap: Making Conscious Contact with God through Meditation* (New York City: Hay House, 2003), 13–14.

20. John Assaraf (author and founder, NeuroGym), in discussion with the author, November 2018.

21. Assaraf, discussion.

22. Deepak Chopra, "5 Steps to Setting Powerful Intentions," The Chopra Center, accessed February 19, 2018, https://chopra.com /articles/5-steps-to-setting-powerful-intentions.

23. Louise Chunn, "The Psychology of the To-Do List—Why Your Brain Loves Ordered Tasks," *Guardian*, May 10, 2017, https:// www.theguardian.com/lifeandstyle/2017/may/10/the-psychology -of-the-to-do-list-why-your-brain-loves-ordered-tasks.

24. David Allen, *Getting Things Done: The Art of Stress-Free Productivity*, rev. ed. (New York: Penguin Books, 2015), 20.

25. Mariano, discussion.

26. Mariano, discussion.

27. Assaraf, discussion.

28. Gail Brenner, *The End of Self-Help: Discovering Peace and Happiness Right at the Heart of Your Messy, Scary, Brilliant Life* (United States: Ananda Press, 2015), 75.

29. Meghan Holohan, "Talk to Yourself Out Loud? Here's Why Experts Say That's a Good Thing," *Today*, February 29, 2016, https://www.today.com/health/talk-yourself-out-loud-here-s-why -experts-say-s-t76531.

30. Mariano, discussion.

31. Glenn Stearns (founder, Stearns Lending, LLC), in discussion with the author, February 2018.

32. Mariano, discussion.

33. Feldman, discussion.

34. Roeglin, discussion.

35. Stearns, discussion.

36. Feldman, discussion.

37. Feldman, discussion.

38. Deborah Rowland, "What's Worse Than a Difficult Conversation? Avoiding One," *Harvard Business Review*, April 8, 2016, https://

hbr.org/2016/04/whats-worse-than-a-difficult-conversation
-avoiding-one.

39. Feldman, discussion.

40. Roeglin, discussion.

41. Roeglin, discussion.

42. Mia Noblet, in discussion with the author, February 2018.

43. Noblet, discussion.

44. Mariano, discussion.

45. Roeglin, discussion.

46. Feldman, discussion.

47. Roeglin, discussion.

48. Amy Cuddy, "I Don't Deserve to Be Here: Presence and the Impostor Syndrome," Lean In, March 3, 2016, https://leanin.org/news-inspiration/overcoming-imposter-syndrome-to-reveal-your-presence/.

49. Roeglin, discussion.

50. Charles D. Martin, *Orange County, Inc.: The Evolution of an Economic Powerhouse* (United States: Chaney-Hall Publishing, 2016).

51. Mariano, discussion.

52. Feldman, discussion.

53. Stearns, discussion.

54. Positive Psychology Program editorial team, "What Is Gratitude and What Is Its Role in Positive Psychology?" *Positive Psychology Program* (blog), February 28, 2017, https://positivepsychologyprogram.com/gratitude-appreciation/.

55. Noblet, discussion.

56. Kim Brown, in discussion with the author, February 2018.